We dance because years ago
your great-great grandmothers
and your great-great grandfathers danced
with the vision of you
strong in their hearts.

And though they are gone from us
they are here in our blood and
here in our breath
lifting from us
to the sky
to the creator.

We dance for our families.
We dance for those who cannot dance.
We dance for our babies and for our elders.
We dance in memory of all those
who have left us and can no longer join us in the dance.

We dance to give of ourselves
for all that has been given to us.

We dance for the coming year.

We dance for the good days to come, not just for us,
but for the whole tribe.

Each place in the dance circle represents a different
time in the year to come.
When the dancing becomes difficult
dance your way through the bad times.
Let there be no bad thoughts in the dance circle.
Each bad thought affects us all in the coming year.
When your heart slows,
When your feet become heavy on the dance floor
Pump your arms
Jump harder
Jump yourself and your people through the bad times.

Dance for your people.
Dance for all living things.

A long time ago, the tribe was close to starvation. The men were having a hard time finding any food. A grandmother, worrying about her grandchildren and all the other people in the tribe, went out into the mountains, into the hills, to pray and to mourn and to worry about what she was going to do. She began to cry and weep, asking the Creator for help and assistance. She sat down and untied her gray hair. As she wept, her tears fell on the ground and turned into bitterroot. For the Flatheads and a lot of tribes in the area, that's why the bitterroot is so important. It is the very first plant in the spring, our main life, what gives us existence.

— told by Joanne Bigcrane

Salish Tradition

For thousands of years the Salish people lived a happy and contented life. They had a special relationship with the earth and all that was around them. The people knew how to take care of themselves and how to help each other.

But long ago, in one village, people were dying and they had no cure. One night the oldest of four brothers had a vision in which he was told to go into the mountains to the east and after three days' travel he would come upon an old man who would help them. So in the morning, the oldest brother told his other brothers of his dream, and they all started on the journey into the mountains. On the evening of the third day, they came upon a place with many lakes, and there they found the lodge of the old man. The old man asked them to enter and instructed his daughter to give them dinner. Then the old man told them, "In the morning we will talk."

In the morning the old man asked the brothers why they had come to see him. The middle brother said, "Our people are sick and dying. We have no medicine to help them. I want to be tall and strong so I can help my brothers and my people." So the old man told him to go out of the lodge, and to turn back and face him. When the brother turned around, he was transformed into a tall tree, a tree that can see all around. "In this way," said the old man, "you can help your people."

The next brother told the old man, "I want to be strong and tough so I can help my people too." And the old man told him to leave the lodge and then turn back and face him. When he did, the old man turned him into a rock that would be strong and endure all kinds of hardship.

And then the old man told the oldest brother to go back to his people and make a little lodge facing east. He should build a fire using his brother the tree, and he should heat his brother the rock in the fire. After bringing the rock into the lodge, he should pray with sincerity. "Always take care of this lodge and pray to me," the old man said. "If you are sincere, then I will help you."

And the old man gave the oldest brother his daughter, who would teach him the proper way to gather and use plants, roots, flowers, and grasses, telling him what is good for this or that sickness. The brothers thanked the old man and left. Each step of the journey home, the young woman instructed them about plants and roots and how to use them to cure illnesses.

— Clarence Woodcock

In those early days the Salish would band together with the Pend Oreille and with other tribes and travel to hunt buffalo. On one of these journeys there was a family, a young boy and his parents. When they went to hunt with the rest of the people, the mother and father were killed, and the boy came home an orphan.

Then he had a vision. He was told to go into the mountains, to pray and to mourn. He stayed there for many days, and one night in a vision he was told that when he grew older he would be taught a new dance, a jump dance or medicine dance, and that when he did this dance, he would be able to help his people. In his vision he was told he would grow to be a strong medicine man and that, when he died, lightning, thunder, and hail would shake the earth. So the young boy went back among his people, and he became a strong medicine man and a prophet known as Shining Shirt.

Shining Shirt was given a vision about the future. He prophesied the coming of fair-skinned men wearing long black robes who would teach the Indians a new way of praying and a new moral law. The Black Robes would bring peace, he predicted, but their arrival would also mean the beginning of the end of all the people who then inhabited the land.

Sacred Encounters

Father De Smet and the Indians of the Rocky Mountain West

Jacqueline Peterson

with Laura Peers

The De Smet Project, Washington State University

in association with the University of Oklahoma Press ◆ Norman and London

Dedicated to Frances Vanderburg, teacher and friend, and to the elders and tradition-bearers of the Coeur d'Alene and Confederated Salish and Kootenai Tribes.

Published in conjunction with the exhibition *Sacred Encounters: Father De Smet and the Indians of the Rocky Mountain West,* organized by Washington State University in collaboration with the Cheney Cowles Museum, and in cooperation with the Jesuit Missouri Province Archives and the Coeur d'Alene and Confederated Salish and Kootenai Tribes. The exhibition was made possible by the support of the National Endowment for the Humanities, the Lilly Endowment, Inc., the Washington Commission for the Humanities, the Montana Committee for the Humanities, the Idaho Humanities Council, and the Missouri Humanities Council.

Publication of the catalogue was made possible with the assistance of the Lilly Endowment, Inc., and the L. J. Skaggs and Mary C. Skaggs Foundation.

Published by the University of Oklahoma Press, Norman, Publishing Division of the University.

Library of Congress Cataloging-in-Publication Data is available.

ISBN 0-8061-2575-6 (cloth)
ISBN 0-8061-2576-4 (paper)

Edited by Suzanne Kotz

Design and production by Katy Homans and Sayre Coombs

Cartography by Allan Jokasaari

Principal photography by Grey Crawford, Joe Mikuliak, Thomas M. Rochford, S.J., and Bill Voxman

Printed and bound in Verona, Italy, by Arnoldo Mondadori Editore

Cover: Nicolas Point, S.J., "Altar in a Tipi," watercolor on paper, ca. 1842–47, Jesuit Missouri Province Archives, St. Louis

Back cover: landscape photograph by Thomas M. Rochford, S.J. Inset: Masseslow, chief of the Kalispel, ca. 1900 (see p. 168)

Dimensions throughout this volume are given in inches and centimeters; height precedes width precedes depth. Objects and artworks are identified according to place of creation, not the birthplace of the artist or maker.

The paper in this book meets the guidelines for permanence and durability of the Committee on Production Guidelines for Book Longevity of the Council on Library Resources, Inc.

1 2 3 4 5 6 7 8 9 10

Contents

Introduction: The Invasion of the Heart

In the beginning, we were very different peoples. We came from totally separate worlds, each of which was very old.

But we were also alike. We were human beings, occupying a portion of this earth that each of us considered to be the very center.

We also shared a belief in a mysterious power beyond ourselves that made all life possible. We called it Amótkan or God; Sumeš or Sacrament. It was everything.

In the wake of the Columbian voyages, the encounter between Christian missionary and Indian sparked both confrontation and dialogue between two sacred worlds. The collision of European and Native American beliefs and values brought about wrenching changes and necessitated entirely new ways of life for native and colonizer alike.

When Pierre-Jean De Smet of Belgium met the Flathead, or Salish, of northwestern Montana in 1841, the encounter between Indian and white in the Western Hemisphere was nearly 350 years old. Although the story of the invasion of the Americas was not new, it assumed many forms. Some were clean and swift, like a knife. Others were subtle, even exquisite, in the masking of their mode of destruction. The most profound was the most intimate: the invasion of the heart.

In the 1830s, despite the encroachments of epidemic disease and white fur traders, the densely folded homeland of the Salish remained a safe haven. Yet, inexplicably, spurred by the prophecies of native visionaries such as Shining Shirt, the Salish and their Nez Perce neighbors began to search for Black Robes, the strange men who wore the cross of the Man-God and did not marry women.

As early as 1811, Catholic Iroquois fur hunters—including Ignace Saxa, or Old Ignace—had migrated from the vicinity of Montreal to the Northern Rockies and intermarried with the Salish and related tribes. These men brought with them an Indianized form of Catholicism, woven from the recollections of their own experience under the Jesuits who had missionized in eastern Canada before being expelled as an order from North America in 1773.

Although the seventeenth-century Jesuit *Relations* reported the torture of priests by the Iroquois, some natives, like Old Ignace—a sacristan in his youth—warmly recalled the Jesuits. Between 1831 and 1837, three successive delegations of Nez Perce, Salish, and Iroquois traveled across the Plains to St. Louis in search of teachers of the new religion. Two delegations

Insula, or Red Feather, Grand Chief and Brave among the Flathead
Nicolas Point, S.J., America, ca. 1841–46
graphite on paper
7¼ x 4¾ (18.4 x 12.1)
De Smetiana Collection, Jesuit Missouri Province Archives, St. Louis

Insula, given the baptismal name of Michel for the archangel of war, was a war chief among the Salish when he first met De Smet at the Rocky Mountain Rendezvous in 1840.

**Pierre-Jean De Smet,
S.J., ca. 1840**
Sacred Heart Mission,
De Smet, Idaho

were led by Old Ignace, who was killed, along with the entire 1837 party, at Ash Hollow near the Nebraska sand hills.

The call of the Rockies was not immediately answered. The Catholic Church and fledgling Jesuit mission and novitiate at the frontier's edge had few men and fewer resources for such a far-flung mission. The romantic saga of previously untutored Indians in search of the white man's God, broadcast in the Protestant press, instead launched the Oregon missions of the Congregationalists (Samuel Parker, 1833), the Methodists (Jason Lee, 1834), and the Presbyterians (Henry Harmon Spalding and Marcus Whitman, 1835–36; Cushing Eells and Elkanah Walker, 1838).

But for the Salish and their Iroquois relatives by marriage, only Jesuits would do. A fourth delegation of two French-speaking Iroquois traveled east again in 1839. This time, at St. Joseph's mission to the Potawatomi at Council Bluffs, they found a man whom the Plains Indians later called "good-hearted," a thirty-eight-year-old Flemish Jesuit named Pierre-Jean De Smet.

For De Smet, the appeal came as a voice crying from the wilderness. He visited the Salish at the Rocky Mountain Rendezvous of 1840, at once fulfilling Shining Shirt's prophecy and sparking native visions of new deities and spirit protectors. The following year, with the blessing of the bishop of St. Louis, De Smet and his European confreres—Nicolas Point, S.J., French artist, architect, and college educator; Gregory Mengarini, S.J., Italian linguist, physician, and musician; and three lay brothers—set out for the Bitterroot Valley of western Montana with visions of their own. St. Mary's mission to the Flathead, modeled after the seventeenth- and eighteenth-century Paraguayan Reductions, became for De Smet the imagined heart of an "empire of Christian Indians," a wilderness kingdom in the uncontaminated reaches of the Rocky Mountains.

A convergence of interest, a conjunction of visions, a shared sense of the miraculous and the interpenetrability of the human and sacred, were not to be mistaken, however, for the desire of the Salish to convert to Christianity. Initially there were similarities of belief upon which to construct a dialogue. The mid-nineteenth-century European Catholic world was caught up in a love affair with the Virgin Mary and a renaissance of romantic piety known as the Devotional Revolution. European Catholics were almost tribal in their devotion to the Holy Family and the saints, and to the values of generosity, community, obedience, and respect for family. Other aspects of Catholic theology and practice resonated or found points of contact with traditional Salish beliefs and practices: the sacramental and transformative power of chant, prayer, and devotional hymns; a sacred calendar associated with sacred colors; the veneration of sacramental objects and sacred sites; the use of water and incense for purification and for transporting prayers to the spirit world; innumerable feast days and sensorially rich ritual dramas and processions; the intercessory powers of saintly guardians and religious specialists (priests); and many of the apostolic values. Both Indian and Catholic worlds depended upon the mediating power of guardian spirits or saints, and both found the way to the sacred through ritual.

For a privileged moment in 1841–42, the mission seemed to prosper. The Salish at St. Mary's settled into a rigorous daily routine of prayer and song, catechism, and agricultural labor. Father Mengarini, who carried a drum, accordion, clarinet, and piccolo across the Plains in his luggage, claimed that within six months his Salish pupils could play the finest European band music of the day. Missions to the neighboring Coeur d'Alene, Pend Oreille, Colville, Kootenai, and Blackfeet tribes were opened in rapid succession.

Nonetheless, from the beginning, the Salish resisted Catholic authoritarianism, the concepts of sin and hell, and the imposition of European social, political, and economic values that directly challenged native norms. The Salish wanted Christian power and protection for their own ends, but they weren't interested in farming or making peace with their Blackfeet enemies. If anything, as Father Mengarini reflected in his memoirs, the prayers of the Flathead "consisted in asking to live a long time, to kill plenty of animals and enemies, and to steal the greatest number of the [enemies'] horses possible."

The mission to the Blackfeet was seen by the Salish as a betrayal. Protestant-Catholic missionary competition and hostility bred confusion and mistrust among neophytes and unbelievers alike. Within scarcely a decade of its founding, St. Mary's mission and the Jesuit missions to the Colville and Blackfeet were closed, their native residents apostatizing due to disease and missionary demands for change far in excess of spiritual conversion. Forced land cessions, war, removal to reservations, and decades of despair would follow. Throughout the latter half of the nineteenth century, missionaries who had accompanied De Smet and those he later recruited continued to breathe life into the Jesuit effort. De Smet's dream of empire, however, was moribund.

After 1847, and for the remainder of his life, De Smet was an advocate for peace. At a time of intense and often violent anti-Catholicism in the United States, De Smet lent his charismatic presence as a trusted military and government emissary in treaty negotiations with reluctant or hostile Indian nations, among whom he was well known. He was a participant at the 1851 Fort Laramie treaty, and he helped to deter the Plateau tribes missionized by the Jesuits from joining their Yakima neighbors in the War of 1858.

His most controversial role involved a mission to the camp of Sitting Bull during the Fort Laramie treaty negotiations of 1868. Although he failed to persuade Sitting Bull of the government's good intentions, he brought in a sufficient number of Sitting Bull's people to secure the treaty and diffuse the threat of immediate war. The Fort Laramie treaty was a hollow victory, however. Government promises were broken within less than a decade, and war, however futile, became the only honorable alternative for the Sioux.

De Smet has been viewed by some as an agent of the United States' expansion. Certainly he never wavered in his belief that the 1868 Fort Laramie treaty was a last best offer, an alternative to extinction for the native peoples of the West. Dying in 1873, he did not see the end of the buffalo days or the demoralization and pain of tribal peoples everywhere during the reservation era. After 1880, both the Catholic Church and the United States government adopted policies bent on destroying Indian identity, Indian culture, Indian religion, and Indian language.

During the late nineteenth century, Indian religion was forced underground. A core of traditional belief and practice persisted, however, reemerging in the late twentieth century as a new message of cultural strength and survival. In a belated gesture of tolerance and apology, the United States Congress in 1978 passed the American Indian Religious Freedom Act, designed to protect the traditional religious sites, beliefs, and practices of all Native Americans.

The last thirty years also have seen the emergence of an Indianized Catholicism in the western United States led by Indian lay men and women. The entwining of Christianity and native belief finds expression in the integration in the Catholic Mass of traditional Indian rituals and sacramentals such as sweetgrass, the drum, and the pipe, as well as in annual pilgrimages to the early Jesuit missions established by De Smet. The grafting of Christianity onto the root stock of traditional native religion is a tentative indication that, after five hundred years, the descendants of European colonizers and the indigenous inhabitants of the Americas may finally have something to say to one another.

The Catholic World

God said, Let us make man in our own image, in the likeness of ourselves, and let them be masters of the fish of the sea, the birds of heaven, the cattle, all the wild beasts and all the reptiles that crawl upon the earth. —Genesis 1:26

Vault of the Church of St. Ignazio
Andrea Pozzo
Rome, ca. 1601–1701
fresco

The light of Christianity is carried to the four continents of the known world by Jesuit missionaries in the fresco of the vault of the Church of St. Ignazio in Rome. The Americas, represented by an Indian woman, occupy one corner of Pozzo's great perspective fresco, which spans more than 1,000 square meters.

Nineteenth-century Roman Catholics believed that their church, presided over by the pope and a hierarchy of priests, was the one true moral and spiritual authority on earth. Their church was a place in which to worship God through the ritual of the Mass with its scent of incense and candle wax, the glow of gold and crystal, and the sound of Gregorian chant and Latin prayers. Beneath the vaulted transept, people reached for heaven and the sacred.

Roman Catholicism had both an institutional and a popular aspect. The church was a comforting place where people sought and found the intercession of a powerful, protective mother, the Virgin Mary, who was seen by believers, along with the angels and saints, as familiar kin to whom they could bring their prayers for help and healing. Church altars and shrines were dedicated to Mary and other saints, and pilgrimages were made to places where miraculous cures and Marian apparitions were reported. Some popular practices, such as the rosary or devotion to the Sacred Heart of Jesus, were approved by the institutional church. Others, like the belief in the healing powers of springs or waterfalls, which had roots in the pagan past, were discouraged as pure superstition.

In De Smet's youth, however, this Catholic world was assaulted by political upheaval. The secular and democratic tides of the French Revolution swept across Catholic Flanders (now Belgium) and De Smet's hometown, Dendermonde, as did the forces of Napoleonic expansion.

Flanders was under French rule from 1797 to 1815, and under Protestant Dutch dominion until 1830. French replaced Flemish as the language of commerce and status, and the virulent anti-Catholicism of the French Revolution led to the closing and ransacking of Flemish monasteries and drove priests into exile. The De Smet family learned to speak and write French, but it was a dangerous time for Pierre-Jean to think about becoming a priest.

Contrary to his aging father's wishes, the twenty-year-old De Smet sailed for America in 1821, secreted out of Amsterdam along with eight other would-be Jesuits. After his arrival at the Jesuit novitiate at White Marsh, Maryland, De Smet wrote to his father, "God has called me; I must follow." De Smet spent most of the 1820s at the Jesuit seminary at Florissant, Missouri, where he became a priest in 1827.

Expansionist Christianity Since the conversion of Paul on the road to Damascus, Christianity has sought to make itself a religion for the world. The revolutionary claim to universality and equality has over the past twenty centuries spawned movements and philosophies of both liberation and oppression. During the age of discovery and exploration,

Christianity became a religion of conquest, and the Society of Jesus, founded by Ignatius of Loyola in 1541, was one of its most fervent standard bearers.

In contrast to other religious orders, the Jesuits wore no particular dress, established no monasteries, followed no rule of hourly prayer and contemplation, and had no particular mission other than the "greater glory of God." The society's deeply committed, tightly disciplined, and highly mobile members rendered service directly to the pope for whatever was most needed in the Counter-Reformation battle with Protestants. Over time, missions and education became the Jesuits' forte.

Often controversial and frequently at odds with kings and popes, and once suppressed as an order, the Jesuits played a major role in extending Catholic missions into the four quarters of the globe. In 1549, less than a decade after the founding of their order, the Jesuits launched one of the largest missionary undertakings in history among the Guaraní Indians of South America. At their height, the Paraguayan Reductions (from *reducere,* the Latin verb meaning to lead back, to bring into the fold) encompassed thirty towns inhabited by more than eighty thousand Indians. Under the paternalistic tutelage of the Jesuits, the Guaraní became town magistrates, sculptors, organ builders, calligraphers, and builders of Baroque cathedrals. The Guaraní towns survived until 1767, when the Jesuits were suppressed as an order and expelled from South America by the Spanish and Portuguese crowns.

The seventeenth- and eighteenth-century Jesuit missions in North America were less successful. The mission to New France, established in 1632 among the Iroquoian-speaking Huron of eastern Canada, was scarcely more than a series of outposts in the agricultural villages of the Huron Confederacy. The Huron Reduction ended in 1649 when, weakened by epidemic disease and conflict between traditional and Christian factions, the Huron Confederacy was destroyed by enemy Iroquois, and its Huron-Wendat members scattered.

Shortly thereafter, the Jesuits established missions among the Iroquois themselves along the St. Lawrence River. It was from these mission communities, particularly Kanewake and Akwesasne near Montreal, that Iroquois voyageurs—who would ultimately settle among the Plateau tribes in the early nineteenth century—were recruited. Kateri Tekakwitha, the first North American Indian candidate for sainthood, came from one of these seventeenth-century Iroquois mission communities.

The slow and fitful progress of the Iroquois mission might have been an apt model for members of the newly restored Society of Jesus after 1815. For the first band of young recruits like Pierre-Jean De Smet, however, who left Europe to minister to the Indians of America, it was the memory of the fabled Paraguayan Reductions that fired the imagination and the soul.

Main Altar of Sint-Gillis-Binnen, Dendermonde, Belgium, 1992
The Church of Sint-Gillis-Binnen was erected in the thirteenth and fourteenth centuries within the walls of the city of Dendermonde, De Smet's birthplace. In 1779 the nave of the old Gothic church was demolished and replaced by three naves in a classical style under one roof separated by columns. The high main altar dates from 1775 to 1800.

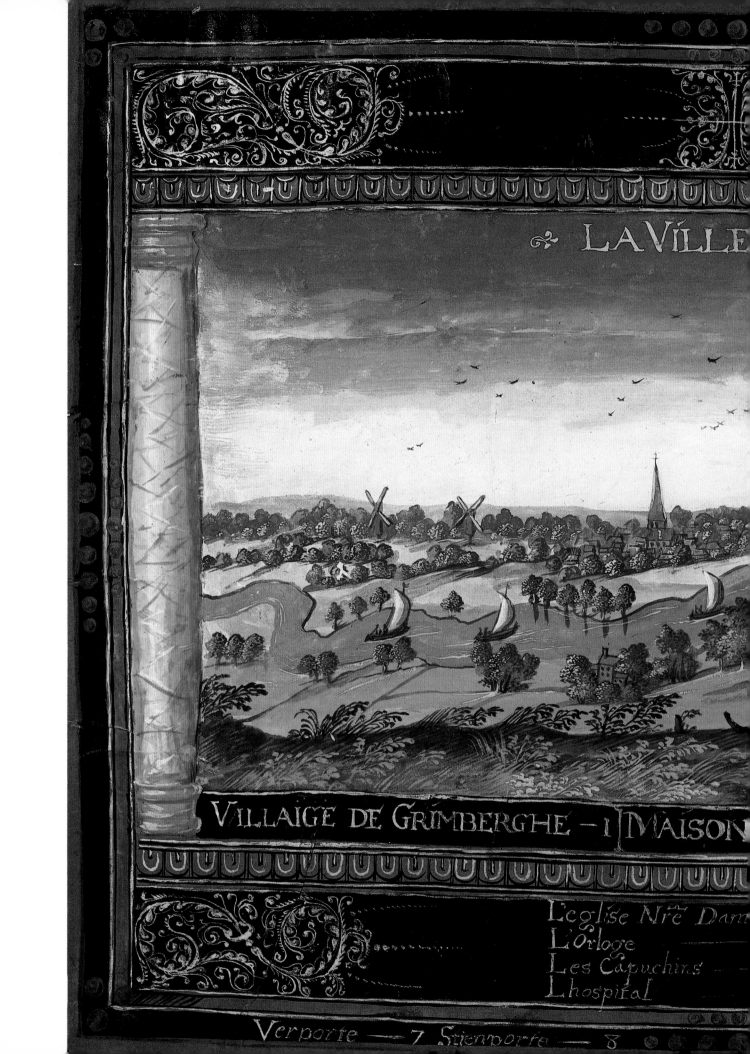

LA VÍLLE

VILLAÍGE DE GRÍMBERGHE — 1 MAÍSON

L'eglíse Nrē Dam
L'Orloge
Les Capuchins
L'hospital

Verporte — 7 Stienporte — 8

E TERMVNDE

E PLAISANCE · Z I

3
4
5
6

"La Ville de Termunde Villaige de Grimberghe"
Adrien de Montigny
Flanders, ca. 1608–1609
from the *Album du Croy*
gouache on parchment
19½ x 25⅝ (49.6 x 65.1)
Österreichische National-bibliothek, Vienna

This lovely seventeenth-century view of Dender-monde, seen from the southwest, shows the towers of the Onze-Lieve-Vrouwekerk (Church of Our Lady), the city hall, the church of Sint-Gillis-Binnen, a windmill, and a town gate. A wooden bridge crossing the Schelde River to the north leads to the village of Grembergen, where the De Smet family had a farm.

Monstrance

H. De Curte/A. Grand, makers
Belgium, ca. 1831–68
Ghent silver, gold plate, brass, glass
26 x 14¹/₂ (66 x 36.8)
Museum of the Western Jesuit Missions, Florissant, Missouri 990.9

The monstrance displays the Blessed Sacrament, or consecrated bread, believed to be Jesus' actual body. During the solemn Forty Hours' Devotion, the monstrance remains on the altar for almost two days so that people may continually show their respect and adoration. In De Smet's time, monstrances were widely used, most frequently at Benediction.

Paten

Flanders, ca. 1800
gold-plated silver
dia. 5¹/₈ (13)
Collection of Jozef Dauwe
Lebbeke, Belgium

After consecrating the host during Mass, the priest placed it on this shallow dish and carried it to the altar rail. Only those who confessed and did penance for their sins were allowed to kneel at the rail and receive Holy Communion.

Chalice

Flanders, ca. 1800
silver, gold-plated silver
h. 9⁷/₈ (22.5)
Collection of Jozef Dauwe,
Lebbeke, Belgium

This simply decorated silver chalice held consecrated wine. Catholics believe in the miracle of transubstantiation, whereby Christ's body and blood are present at the Mass in the symbols of bread and wine. In De Smet's day, only the priest drank from the cup.

Chalice Spoon

Flanders, ca. 1800
gold-plated silver
3¹/₄ x ³/₄ x ³/₄ (8.2 x 1.8 x 1.8)
Collection of Jozef Dauwe,
Lebbeke, Belgium

Priests used the chalice spoon to add a few drops of water to the wine when preparing bread and wine during Catholic Mass.

Censor

B. L. Gyselyck, maker
Ghent, 1783
repoussé silver, copper,
iron, silver-plated brass
h. 9½ (42.1)
Kerkfabriek Onze-Lieve-
Vrouwekerk, Dender-
monde, Belgium

The incense that burned
in this censor, from the
Church of Our Lady in
Dendermonde, purified
and sanctified the altar
and people during Catho-
lic Mass. Incense trans-
ported petitions heaven-
ward, like the smoke of
burning cedar and juni-
per, which purified the
Salish and lifted their
prayers to the spirit
world.

Missale Romanum Ex Decreto Sacro Sancti

Antwerp, 1765
leather, paper, gold, silk
14 x 9¾ x 3⅛ (35.5 x
24.7 x 7.9)
Collection of Jozef Dauwe,
Lebbeke, Belgium

Christianity is based on
the sacred written text of
the Bible. In the Catholic
tradition, church teach-
ings are also regarded
as authoritative. In De
Smet's day, only priests
read church teachings
printed in Latin. This altar
book was the only text
approved for the Roman
Catholic Mass according
to a decree of Pope
Urbanus VIII (1568–
1644).

Altar Cross

Flanders, ca. 1750–1800
ebony veneer, boxwood,
brass, plaster, paint
38½ x 15 (97.7 x 38.2)
V.Z.W.D. Begijnhof van
Dendermonde, Dender-
monde, Belgium
79.258.512

This typical Belgian cru-
cifix, signifying Jesus'
death and resurrection,
would have been the
most prominent symbol
on a Catholic altar. The
suffering body nailed to
the cross empha-
sized Jesus' sac-
rifice for the sins
and salvation
of all people.

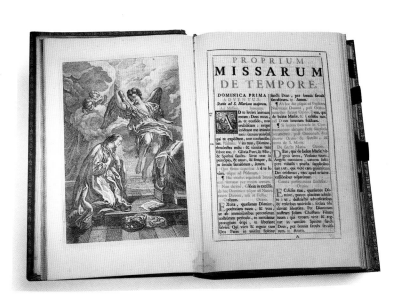

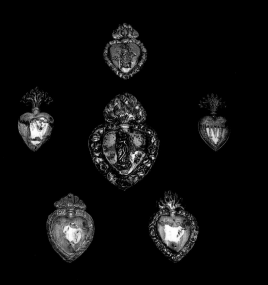

Ex-voto Hearts
Belgium, ca. 1800–1900
silver, silver-plated brass
avg. 3¹/₄–6¹/₈ x 1⁷/₈–4
(9.5–15.5 x 4.7–10.2)
Collection of Jozef Dauwe,
Lebbeke, Belgium
Collection of Dom. Bernard Daeleman o.s.b.,
Dendermonde, Belgium

Flemish Catholics in De
Smet's day typically gave
silver hearts as ex-voto
offerings to the Virgin
Mary. The heart shape
was a sign of the love
and familiarity felt for
Mary.

**Virgin Mary Holding
the Christ Child**
Flanders, ca. 17th or 18th
century
wood, polychrome
31 x 10¹/₂ x 8 (78.8 x
26.7 x 20.3)
Collection of Jozef Dauwe,
Lebbeke, Belgium

Simple statues like this
one, here displayed on
a replica of a Baroque
Marion altar, typically were
clothed in brocades or
damask robes. After 1850,
such statues often wore a
crown and carried a scep-
ter, evidence of a growing
emphasis on Mary as the
Queen of Heaven.

Candlesticks
Dendermonde, Belgium,
ca. 1750–1800
brass
h. 23 ¹/₈ (59.5)
Kerkfabriek Onze-Lieve-
Vrouwekerk, Dender-
monde, Belgium

Ex-voto Painting
François Jacquin
Brussels, 1803
oil on textile
42⅛ x 33⅜ (107 x 84.8)
Kerkfabriek Onze-
Lieve-Vrouwekerk,
Dendermonde, Belgium

Portraits of young girls
presenting their hearts
to the Virgin Mary were
hung adjacent to the
Marian altar of many Bel-
gian churches. Parents
consecrated the life of
a child to the Virgin in
thanksgiving for an-
swered prayers.

Flight of the Holy Family
Michael Cabbaye
Flanders, ca. 1722
etching, ink, watercolor
or gouache on parchment
4³/₄ x 3¹¹/₁₆ (12.1 x 9.3)
Collection of Jozef Dauwe,
Lebbeke, Belgium

Holy Family at Work
Paris, ca. 1800
copper engraving, ink,
watercolor or gouache
on paper
16¹/₁₆ x 10⁵/₈ (42.2 x 27)
Collection of Jozef Dauwe,
Lebbeke, Belgium

Humanistic portrayals of
the Holy Family at home
and at work made Mary
and Joseph more acces-
sible than they had ap-
peared in the religious
art of previous centuries.
In the mid-nineteenth
century, devotions to
the Holy Family grew in
popularity.

St. Anthony of Padua
Cornelius De Boudt
Antwerp, ca. 1700–35
engraving, watercolor or
gouache on paper
4³/₄ x 3³/₄ (12.1 x 7)
Collection of Jozef Dauwe,
Lebbeke, Belgium

Flaming Heart
Flanders, ca. 1700–35
gouache or watercolor
on paper
3⁵/₈ x 2⁷/₁₆ (9.1 x 6.1)
Collection of Jozef Dauwe,
Lebbeke, Belgium

Scapular
Belgium, ca. 1850–1900
cotton, cotton flannel,
embroidery floss, flat
braid, ink
3⁵/₈ x 2³/₄ (9.5 x 7)
Collection of Dom Ber-
nard Daeleman o.s.b.,
Dendermonde, Belgium

Wearing this scapular
around the neck or
pinned to a shirt publicly
expressed devotion to
the Virgin Mary and
served as an inward
stimulus to Christian life.
Although members of
religious orders wore
scapulars from the thir-
teenth century, the cus-
tom did not achieve
widespread popularity
as a devotion until the
nineteenth century.

Holy Water Font
Europe, 18th century
cast metal, copper,
brass plating, paint
9³/₈ x 3³/₄ x 3 (23.5 x
9.5 x 7.6)
Museum of the Western
Jesuit Missions, Floris-
sant, Missouri 991.41

This small holy water
font, in the form of an
angel holding a chalice
with a host in her left
hand, was meant to be
hung on a wall at home.
Family members sought
blessings and protection
by crossing themselves
with holy water from the
font upon arising and
before bed.

De Smet's Rosary
Europe, ca. 1850
silver, ebonized wood,
walnut beads, metal
l. 15³/₈ (39.5)
Museum of the Western
Jesuit Missions, Floris-
sant, Missouri 991.5

This simple rosary, a
popular devotion to the
Virgin Mary, is believed
to have belonged to De
Smet. In the nineteenth
century, people often
prayed the rosary during
Mass as well as at home.

**Neighborhood Shrine
near Dendermonde,
Belgium, 1992**
Fishermen prayed and
left devotions at this
nineteenth-century
chapel alongside the
Schelde River. Flemish
roadside shrines like this
were often dedicated
to the patron saint of a
particular neighborhood
or family.

Judocus De Smet
unknown artist
Belgium, 1825
oil on textile
38⅝ x 33 (97.8 x 83.5)
Stedelijke Musea,
Dendermonde, Belgium
1167

The elder De Smet, a
prominent shipping mer-
chant of Dendermonde,
fathered twenty-two
children. Pierre-Jean,
born in 1801, was among
the youngest. This por-
trait of Judocus De Smet
holding a letter, perhaps
from his son, was made
when Judocus was
eighty-eight years old.

**De Smet's Letter to
His Father**
White Marsh, Maryland,
October 18, 1821
Pierre Jean De Smet
Papers, Washington State
University Libraries,
Pullman 537.2.2

De Smet and his fellow
novices arrived in Amer-
ica in October 1821 after
more than a month at
sea. From the Jesuit novitiate at White Marsh,
Maryland, De Smet
penned an apology to
his aging father for his
clandestine departure
from Belgium, saying he
had no choice but to
follow God's call. Mail
delivery was slow, and
two years passed before
young De Smet received
an answer.

List of Priests Expelled from Belgium
France, 1798
ink on hand-laid paper
14 x 18 (35.6 x 45.7)
Collection of Jozef Dauwe,
Lebbeke, Belgium

All priests who refused
to swear fidelity in 1791
to the French revolution-
ary constitution were
forced out of Belgium;
many were imprisoned
and condemned to forced
labor. De Smet's older
brother, Jean-Baptiste, a
diocesan priest, was ex-
iled to the Island of Ré
and had to be ransomed
by his father.

Pierre-Jean De Smet
unknown artist
Belgium, ca. 1833–37
oil on textile
36³/₈ x 29³/₄ (92.4 x 75.5)
Stedelijke Musea,
Dendermonde, Belgium
1163

An artist probably made
this portrait during De
Smet's four-year stay in
Belgium in the 1830s.
He had returned to beg
money and recruit nov-
ices for the Jesuits in
Missouri, but health
problems forced him to
remain in Belgium.

Mounted Celestial Globe

Willem Blaeu
Netherlands, ca. 1696
wood, paper, varnish,
inks, brass
39½ x 35½ (100 x 90)
Museum of the Western
Jesuit Missions, Floris-
sant, Missouri 991.38

This pair of Blaeu globes
reflects the state of geographical knowledge
among European cartog-
raphers after more than
a century of exploration
and discovery. The globes
also strikingly portray
the division in western
European thought be-
tween heaven and earth,
between the supernat-
ural and the natural.

The celebrated Dutch
cartographer Willem
Blaeu (1571–1638) first
published 68-centimeter
globes in 1616–17. His
son Joan reissued the
globes between 1645 and
1648, and after his death
the plates passed from
hand to hand until they
came into the possession
of Jacob de la Feuille in
1696.

The celestial globe
with de la Feuille's im-
print dates from 1696.
There is only one other
like it, in the collection
of the Scheepvaart Mu-
seum, Amsterdam. This is
the only known pair of
Blaeu globes in the West-
ern Hemisphere.

Mounted Terrestrial Globe

Willem Blaeu
Netherlands, ca. 1696
wood, paper, varnish,
inks, brass
39½ x 35½ (100 x 90)
Museum of the Western
Jesuit Missions, Floris-
sant, Missouri 991.39

Seal of the Society of Jesus
Rome, ca. 1605
fresco
Rooms of St. Ignatius,
Church of Gesù, Rome

This fresco of the seal of
the Society of Jesus was
uncovered in a niche of
a bricked-up doorway
at the entrance to the
rooms of Ignatius of Loy-
ola in Rome. The fresco
probably dates from
1605, when the rooms
became a shrine.

Ignatius of Loyola, a
Spanish courtier from the
Basque Mountains, was
born in 1491, the year
before Columbus's land-
fall in North America. A
self-described pilgrim for
Christ, Ignatius was one
of Europe's first modern
men, a product of the
Renaissance and the age
of European expansion.

*Exercitia Spiritualia
S. P. Ignatii Loyolæ*
Antwerp, 1635
ink, paper
5⅝ x 3¾ x ⅝ (14.2 x
9.5 x 1.6)
St. Louis University
Archives, Pius XII Memo-
rial Library

Ignatius of Loyola made
the first notes for the
Spiritual Exercises at
Manresa, Spain, during
more than a year of
convalescence and spiri-
tual transformation after
being wounded in 1521
at the battle of Pamp-
lona. First printed in 1548
in Latin, the Spiritual
Exercises serve as the
Jesuits' primary text, the
source and center of
Jesuit spirituality.

Jesuit Rings
France, ca. 1750
brass
dia. ¾ (2)
Minnesota Historical So-
ciety, Archaeological Collections, St. Paul 388.50.2,
388.51.3

These Jesuit rings may
have been received as
rewards for a good cat-
echism, or they may have
been acquired from
French or British fur
traders, who imported
them into the upper
Great Lakes in the seven-
teenth and eighteenth
centuries.

*Relation de ce qui
s'est passé en la
Nouvelle France en
l'année 1635*
Paul le Jeune, S.J.
Paris, 1636
paper, leather, gilt
6³⁄₁₆ x 4¼ x ¾ (15.7 x
10.7 x 2)
Clements Library, Univer-
sity of Michigan, Ann
Arbor C RJ 1636 LE JEUNE

The Jesuit missionaries
to New France submitted
yearly accounts to their
superior. Known as *rela-
tions*, the reports were
printed in France, to be
read by other Jesuits and
wealthy patrons of the
missions. This relation
for 1635–36 was written
in part by Father Jean
de Brebeuf, who was
martyred in 1649. It tells
of the Jesuits' early work
among the Huron Con-
federacy and of the ter-
rible effects of European
diseases upon the Huron.

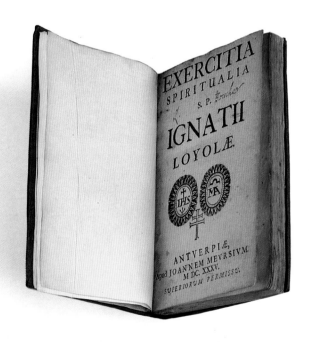

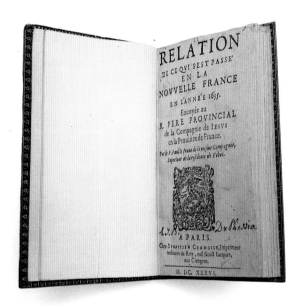

Votive Wampum
Huron-Wendat, ca. 1678
shell, rawhide, porcupine
quills
8¹/₈ x 71⁷/₈ (18 x 183)
Tresor de la Cathédrale
de Chartres, Chartres,
France

Iroquoian people used
"wampum"—beads made
from shell—to record
important events in sym-
bolic form. Following the
destruction of the Huron
missions in 1649, survi-
vors fled to the village of
Lorette in Quebec. This
belt was made there by
Huron converts as an ex-
voto to the Virgin Mary.
It was taken to the ca-
thedral at Chartres in
1698.

**Martyrdom of the
Jesuits in New
France**
François-Joseph Bressani
France, ca. 1657
engraving
20³/₄ x 30¹/₂ (52.7 x 77.8)
Bibliothèque Nationale,
Départment des Cartes et
Plans, Paris GE DD 2987
B(8580)

In the 1640s the Huron
were repeatedly attacked
by their Iroquois enemies
and finally forced to flee.
The Iroquois captured six
Jesuit priests in these
raids, three of whom
were tortured to death in
accord with the Iroquois
custom for worthy male
captives. Father François-
Joseph Bressani, who
survived Iroquois torture,
created this image of the
martyrdom of Fathers
Gabriel Lalemant and
Jean de Brebeuf, whose
deaths marked the end
of the dream of a Huron
Reduction.

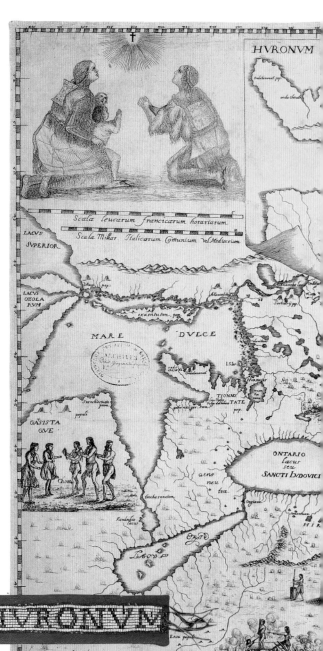

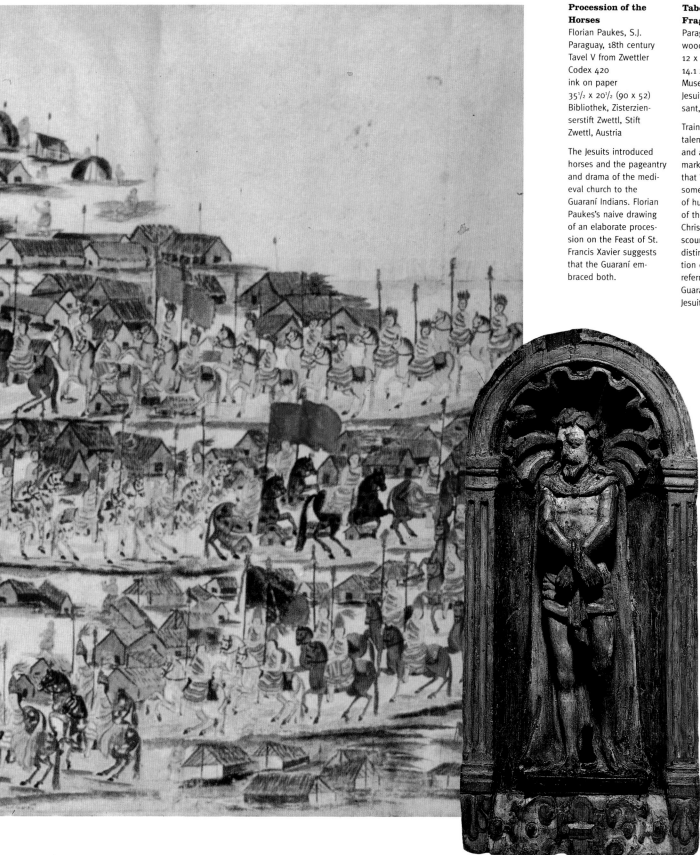

Procession of the Horses
Florian Paukes, S.J.
Paraguay, 18th century
Tavel V from Zwettler
Codex 420
ink on paper
35½ x 20½ (90 x 52)
Bibliothek, Zisterzienserstift Zwettl, Stift Zwettl, Austria

The Jesuits introduced horses and the pageantry and drama of the medieval church to the Guaraní Indians. Florian Paukes's naive drawing of an elaborate procession on the Feast of St. Francis Xavier suggests that the Guaraní embraced both.

Tabernacle Door Fragment
Paraguay, ca. 1600–50
wood, paint
12 x 5½ x 2¼ (30.5 x 14.1 x 5.8)
Museum of the Western Jesuit Missions, Florissant, Missouri 991.9

Trained by the Jesuits, talented Guaraní artists and architects built a remarkable world of beauty that Voltaire called "in some ways the triumph of humanity." This carving of the "Man of Sorrows," Christ bound and scourged, illustrates the distinctive artistic tradition of the Reductions referred to as mestizo or Guaraní-Baroque, or Jesuit-Guaraní Baroque.

A Time of Prophets: The Salish World in Transition

Before whites arrived, the Salish and their Coeur d'Alene, Spokane, Pend Oreille, and Kalispel neighbors lived a contented life. In the mountain meadows and river valleys of present-day northwestern Montana and northern Idaho, they hunted deer and moose, fished for salmon, and gathered roots and berries. Village members were usually kin, theft was rare, and almost everyone had *sumeš,* or medicine power.

The Bitterroot River near Stevensville, Montana, 1992

This portion of the Bitterroot River was close to the original site of St. Mary's mission and to the main winter village of the Salish. To the Salish people the Bitterroot Mountains were known as the Red Mountains.

The Indian view of the world was profoundly religious. Unlike the grizzly and eagle, human beings were frail. Their lives depended upon blessings, or medicines, received from guardian animal spirits who came to them through visions and dreams. Spiritual power, both beneficent and malevolent, was everywhere. Animals could talk to their human relatives, and words, like sacred songs, had the power to transform and heal as well as to kill.

Although food was sometimes scarce, the people depended upon plant and animal species that returned each year like visiting family. Beginning with the bitterroot's arrival in May, each plant and animal relative was received with prayer and ceremony. Spawning fish and new roots came in spring, wildfowl and berries in summer, fat deer in autumn, and bison and moose in winter.

The richness of the extensive buffalo herds of the Great Plains attracted native peoples who lived nearby, and after the introduction of the horse in the mid-eighteenth century, the bison became easier to reach. The buffalo country was claimed by the Blackfeet, who not only outnumbered and outgunned their longtime Salish enemies but raided their horses. In Salish, *tcinés-geílci,* the verb for "going to war," means "stealing horses." But the Salish wanted the bison, and even though it meant fighting the Blackfeet, they crossed the Rocky Mountains in winter and summer to hunt on the open Plains. The people relied on medicine songs and powers given by guardian spirits and on their own bravery to protect them.

Trade and Contact Long before whites arrived, people from the Pacific Coast, the desert Southwest, the Basin, the Rocky Mountains, and the Plains traveled hundreds of miles on foot to trade fairs at the Dalles on the Columbia, at Spokane Falls, at Pierre's Hole, and at the juncture of the Yellowstone and Missouri rivers in Mandan country. There native people bartered goods such as shells, baskets, woven bags, dried corn, hide parfleches, and buffalo robes. Even enemy tribes engaged in trade, as recorded in a remarkable sketch of a Salish band swapping goods with a friendly Blackfeet band (see p. 77).

When Lewis and Clark crossed the Rockies in 1805, the Shoshones told them that they could travel to the Spanish settlements in the Southwest in just ten days. Through dealings with the Shoshone, the Plateau tribes obtained horses, perhaps the most important trade item in North America. With the horse came Spanish-style saddles with high pommels, the lasso and the whip, mission bells and crosses, and a story about a Man-God who rose from the dead.

Influences also came from the Northeast. The Hudson's Bay and North West companies hoped to find beaver "as thick as the blades of grass" in the Rockies. They arrived among the Salish by 1809, bringing with them the first guns. They also brought employees of many nations, cultures, and beliefs. Iroquois voyageurs introduced an Indian version of Christianity; Métis, Cree, and Ojibwa trappers brought floral beadwork; the Scots even brought their bagpipes.

Beginning in the early 1800s, American fur traders began holding their own trade fairs, or "rendezvous." Every imaginable trade good could be found at the rendezvous, along with people from across the Plains and Plateau, joined by British and American traders and their Indian employees.

The introduction of Europeans and their trade goods brought profound change. European diseases killed over half the tribal people of the Northern Rockies between 1780 and 1810, and epidemics continued to strike throughout the next half-century. Alcohol introduced by traders devastated native people. Although the European goods seemed exciting and made life easier, the balance of trade after 1800 was uneven. Indian people lost more than they gained.

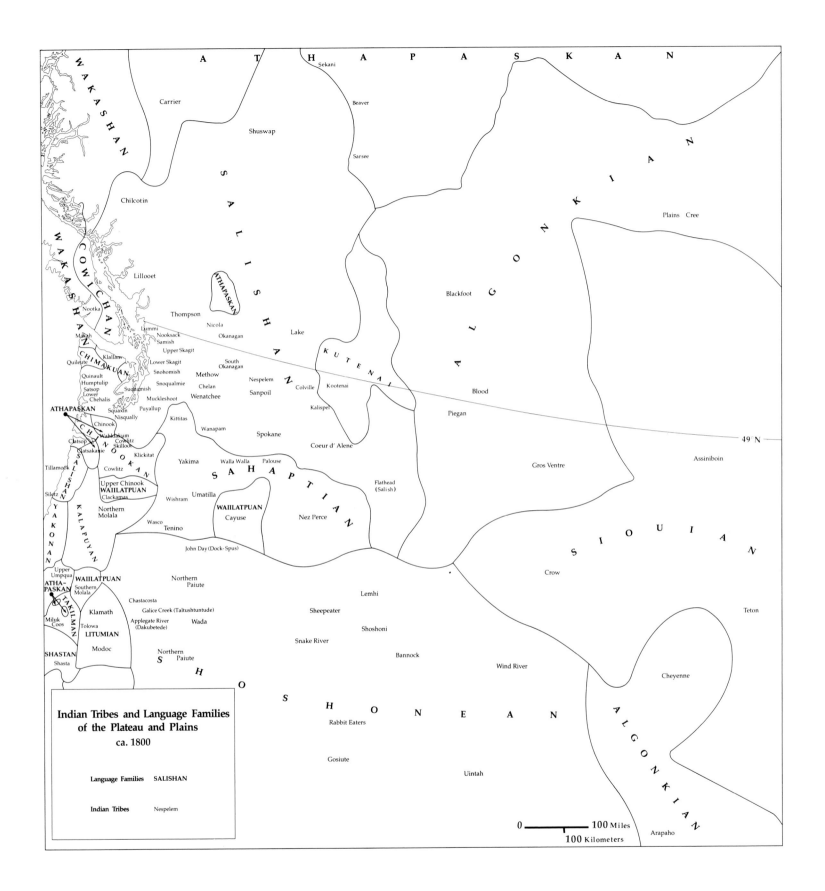

**Indian Tribes and Language Families
of the Plateau and Plains
ca. 1800**

Language Families   SALISHAN

Indian Tribes   Nespelem

0 ——— 100 Miles
100 Kilometers

ATHAPASKAN

WAKASHAN

Carrier

Sekani

Beaver

Sarsee

Shuswap

Chilcotin

Plains   Cree

A L G O N K I A N

Blackfoot

ATHAPASKAN

Lillooet

Nootka

Thompson

Nicola

Lummi

Nooksack

Samish

Upper Skagit

Lower Skagit

Klallam

Quileute

Quinault

Humptulip

Satsop

Lower

Chehalis

Snohomish

Suquamish

Snoqualmie

Muckleshoot

Squaxin

Nisqually

Chinook

ATHAPASKAN

Clatsop

Wahkiakum

Cowlitz

Skilloot

Natsakanie

Klickitat

Tillamook

Cowlitz

Upper Chinook

WAIILATPUAN

Clackamas

Northern

Molala

Siletz

Wasco

Tenino

John Day (Dock-Spus)

Upper

Umpqua

**ATHA-
PASKAN**

WAIILATPUAN

Southern

Molala

Chastacosta

Galice Creek (Taltushtuntude)

Applegate River

(Dakubetede)

Klamath

Wada

Tolowa

LITUMIAN

Miluk

Coos

Modoc

SHASTAN

Shasta

Northern

Paiute

Northern

Paiute

Klamath

Kittitas

Wanapam

Yakima

Spokane

Walla Walla

Palouse

Umatilla

Wishram

SAHAPTIAN

Cayuse

Nez Perce

Methow

Chelan

Wenatchee

South

Okanagan

Okanagan

Lake

Nespelem

Colville

Sanpoil

Kootenai

Kalispel

Coeur d' Alene

K U T E N A I

Blood

Piegan

49 N

Flathead

(Salish)

Gros Ventre

Assiniboin

Crow

S I O U I A N

Teton

Lemhi

Sheepeater

Shoshoni

Snake River

Bannock

Wind River

Cheyenne

Rabbit Eaters

S H O S H O N E A N

Gosiute

Uintah

Arapaho

A L G O N K I A N

S A L I S H A N

CHIMAKUAN

COWICHAN

WAKASHAN

CHINOOK

KALAPUYAN

YAKONAN

TAKILMAN

S A H A P T I A N

Flat Bag
Plateau (Spokane),
ca. 1875–1900
hemp, grass, Indian
tanned leather
29¹¹/₁₆ x 23¹/₂ (75.4 x
59.6)
Cheney Cowles Museum,
Spokane, Washington
1070.176

Camas and bitterroot not
immediately cooked and
eaten were stored inside
bags woven of twined
natural fiber and embroi-
dered with grass. A bag
like this normally took a
skilled woman more than
a week to make.

**Digging Stick and
Handle**
Plateau (Nez Perce),
ca. 1890–1910
wood, antler
l. 29¹/₂ (73.4)
National Park Service,
Nez Perce National His-
torical Park, Spalding,
Idaho NPNHP 159,
NPNHP 18715

In early summer, when
the high prairies burst
into bloom with blue
camas flowers, parties
of women and children
returned to their family
camas grounds to dig
the succulent roots with
sticks like this one. The
roots were then slowly
steamed in earthen ov-
ens for immediate con-
sumption or sun-dried
for later use.

Camas in Bloom on the Flathead Reservation near Evaro, Montana, 1992

The camas root was a principal food of the Salish people in the nineteenth century. Salish women still dig camas when it flowers in early June and serve its roots at family and community feasts throughout the year.

20

Campement du Soir.

Setting up Evening Camp (detail)
Nicolas Point, S.J.
America, ca. 1841–47
ink on paper
4¼ x 6⅞ (10.8 x 16.5)
De Smetiana Collection, Jesuit Missouri Province Archives, St. Louis
IX-C9-92

Women took pride in their ability to manage, move, and set up camp. It took a woman about fifteen minutes to erect her family's lodge after a day's journey. Europeans often considered Indian women as "beasts of burden," but in truth everyone worked hard. Women maintained considerable authority in camp, and their skills were respected.

Family of Dolls
Plateau (Coeur d'Alene), late 19th century
Indian tanned leather, trade cloth, hair, sinew, glass seed beads, wood, feathers
h. male: 25 (63.5), female: 24⅜ (62), cradleboard: 17 (43.2)
Department of Anthropology, Smithsonian Institution, Washington, D.C.
213.522, 213.523, 213.524

A Coeur d'Alene girl might have played camp with this family of dolls made by her mother or other fond adult. Dolls helped to socialize Plateau children, who learned by watching adults and imitating them in play. Girls commonly kept their beloved dolls with them, even after marriage.

Catching Waterfowl (detail)
Nicolas Point, S.J.
America, ca. 1841–47
graphite on paper
4 x 6⅞ (10.2 x 17.8)
De Smetiana Collection,
Jesuit Missouri Province
Archives, St. Louis
IX-C9-41

Ducks were so numerous at some lakes and swamps that they could be killed by hand.

Hunting Wolves
Nicolas Point, S.J.
America, ca. 1841–47
ink on paper
4¼ x 7 (10.8 x 17.8)
De Smetiana Collection,
Jesuit Missouri Province
Archives, St. Louis
IX-C9-58

The most successful hunters were those who had been given powerful hunting medicines by animal spirits who visited them during a vision quest, a spiritual retreat in which a man or woman went alone into the mountains, fasted, and prayed for assistance. All hunters respected the souls of the animals who gave themselves up to humans. When an animal was killed, a prayer offering was made, and the carcass was treated with reverence.

Split-horn Headdress
Plateau (Flathead),
pre-1897
Indian tanned leather, fur, horn, wool, other textile, thread, metal, brass buttons, hackle feather
18 x 15 x 9 (45.7 x 38.1 x 22.9)
Field Museum of Natural History, Chicago 51791

Made of the fur of bear, bison, mountain sheep, and ermine, and crowned by split, carved bison horn, this headdress incorporates a number of powerful animal spirits. When collected on the Flathead Reservation in 1897, a man used it as a dance bonnet and probably as a ceremonial piece as well.

Le Père, la mère et la petite fille appercevant un troupeau de buffles.

Father, Mother, and Daughter on the Hunt
Nicolas Point, S.J.
America, ca. 1841–47
ink on paper
4¼ x 6½ (10.8 x 16.5)
De Smetiana Collection,
Jesuit Missouri Province
Archives, St. Louis
IX-C9-106

A family sights a herd of bison. Women were excellent riders, and they accompanied men on the hunt to butcher the animals and dry the meat for storage.

Return of the Hunter
Nicolas Point, S.J.
America, ca. 1841–47
ink on paper
4¼ x 7 (10.8 x 17.8)
De Smetiana Collection,
Jesuit Missouri Province
Archives, St. Louis
IX-C9-59

For most of the year, the Salish and their neighbors ate well from plentiful supplies. Winters could be lean, and then women and children fasted to give food to the hunters. For this family, hunger is over.

Incised Parfleche
Plains or Plateau,
19th century
buffalo hide, Indian
tanned leather
20³/₄ x 13³/₈ x 1¹/₂ (52.7
x 34 x 3.8)
Cheney Cowles Museum,
Spokane, Washington
1780.916

Although men did all of
the hunting and butcher-
ing, women owned the
food once it came into
the lodge and were re-
sponsible for drying and
storing it. They made
rawhide cases, or par-
fleches, to hold dried
meat. Usually women
painted designs on
parfleches; only a hand-
ful survive such as this
one, which was deco-
rated by cutting the de-
sign into the hide.

Headstall Strips
Plains or Plateau, col-
lected by Pierre-Jean
De Smet, 1859
Indian tanned leather,
porcupine quills, glass
seed beads, cotton,
silk, sinew
13³/₄ x 1¹/₂ (34.9 x 3.9)
Private collection,
Belgium

Horses became so impor-
tant to Plateau peoples
that women made special
ornaments for them. The
making of these head-
stall strips required great
knowledge of hide tan-
ning and porcupine quill-
work. Women decorated
saddle blankets and
made fancy martingales,
cruppers, and headstalls
for their favorite horses.

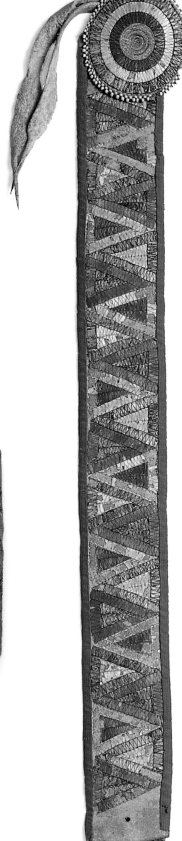

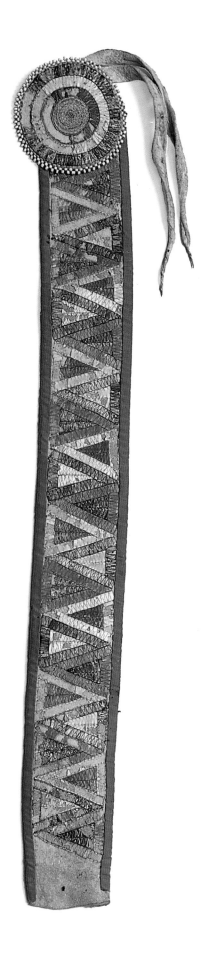

Travail des femmes après la Chasse

Women's Work after the Hunt (detail)
Nicolas Point, S.J.
America, ca. 1841–47
ink on paper
4¼ x 6½ (10.8 x 16.5)
De Smetiana Collection,
Jesuit Missouri Province
Archives, St. Louis
IX-C9-94

Women dried and stored meat, and tanned hides for robes, clothing, and lodge covers. If men's hunting skills satisfied immediate hunger, women's skills as meat processors and as gatherers of the more predictable harvests of roots and berries brought the people through the long months after the hunt.

Beaded Moccasins
Plateau, collected by
Jean-Pierre De Smet, 1859
Indian tanned leather,
rawhide, wool, glass seed
beads, cotton, sinew
10¾ x 3⅞ x 6 (27.3 x
9.9 x 15.2)
Private collection,
Belgium

These moccasins have hard rather than soft soles. Hard soles became necessary as Plateau people spent more time hunting bison on the Plains, which were covered with prickly pear cactus. The beaded design is evidence of the adaptation by Plateau women of eastern Woodlands double-curve and floral designs.

Fringed Medicine Case
Plateau (Flathead), mid-
19th century
Indian tanned leather,
rawhide, leather, wool
13 x 4 (33 x 10.2)
Field Museum of Natural
History, Chicago 51774

The Flathead, or Salish, peoples shared with many Plains tribes this style of flat rawhide pouch made to hold sacred objects. In camp, a man's medicine case and his weapons ordinarily hung on a tripod outside the lodge. This pouch was collected from the Flathead in 1897.

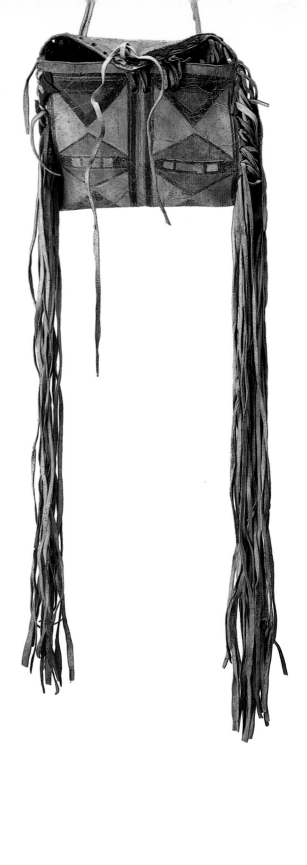

Woman's Fringed Dress
Plateau (Nez Perce),
mid-19th century
Indian tanned leather,
glass pony beads, sinew,
dentalium shells, pig-
ment
53 x 78½ (135 x 200)
Thaw Collection, courtesy
New York State Historical
Association, Cooperstown

A special dress engaged
the talents of an entire
family. Female relatives
designed, beaded, and
sewed the dress. Male
relatives hunted for the
deerskins and traded for
the dentalium shells and
black and white pony
beads, which were ex-
pensive. It might have
taken a year to trade for
the ornaments on this
dress.

Cradleboard with Pony Beads
Plateau (Nez Perce),
ca. 1836–45
Indian tanned leather,
dentalium shells, glass
pony beads, elk teeth,
sinew
30 x 9³/₈ x 7½ (76.2 x
23.9 x 19)
Ohio Historical Society,
Columbus 1994-16

Indian women who still
use cradleboards say
that babies cry when
they are removed. The
snug wrappings made
children feel secure, and
moss padding kept bot-
toms dry. Whether carried
on a mother's back, hung
from a saddle, or sus-
pended from a tree limb,
a cradleboard kept a
busy woman's hands free
and her child close by.

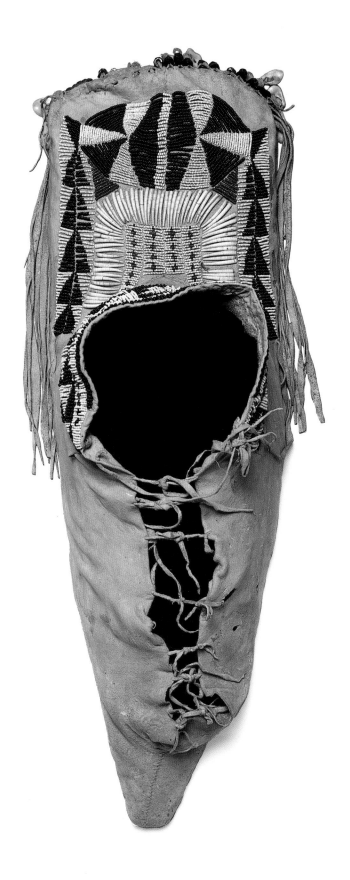

The Game of Al-kol-lock Chualpay Indians Columbia River

Gambling Set
Plateau, 19th century
deer bone, Indian tanned
leather
3 x ¾ (7.6 x 2)
Cheney Cowles Museum,
Spokane, Washington
KING 1970 #45

Stick game, or hand
game, was played by all
Plateau tribes. Players
pitted their medicine
powers against one an-
other in a sleight-of-hand
game that could last all
night and result in the
loss of a man's posses-
sions. A player who failed
to guess the hand that
held the bone marked
with sinew gave up a
stick, or counter, to the
opposing side. When one
side had all the sticks,
the game was over.

**"Game of Al-kol-lock,
Columbia River"**
Paul Kane
America, 1847
graphite and watercolor
on paper
5½ x 9 (14 x 22.9)
Stark Museum of Art,
Orange, Texas 31.78/77,
WWC 78

Like the hand game
played with bones and
sticks, *al-kol-lock*, or the
hoop and arrow game,
was an occasion for gam-
bling among Plateau
men.

**Hoop and Stick Game:
Hoops**
Plateau (Flathead), 19th
century
metal, Indian tanned
leather, glass beads
dia. 3, 2⅝ (7.1, 6.7)
Field Museum of Natural
History, Chicago 51793.1,
51793.2

Plateau people played
games as a serious but
enjoyable way to build
manual skills, dexterity,
and steadiness under
pressure. In this hoop
and arrow game, male
contestants aimed their
arrows at the spot where
they judged the hoops
would stop rolling. For
young boys, this became
a "war game," in which
they practiced throwing
their arrows through the
rolling hoop's center.

Children Playing with Tops on Ice
Nicolas Point, S.J.
America, ca. 1841–47
oil on paper
3¹⁵/₁₆ x 6³/₁₆ (10 x 15.8)
Archives des Jésuites,
St-Jérôme, Québec
BO-43-18

Traditional Top and Whip
Henry Magee
Plains (Blackfeet), 1942
wood, Indian tanned
leather
top: 2⁷/₁₆ x 1⁵/₈ (6.2 x
4.1), whip: l. 39¹/₂ (100.3)
John C. Ewers Collection,
Arlington, Virginia

Indian children enjoyed
a great deal of freedom
and spent much of their
time outdoors playing
with other children. Older
male relatives made toys
like this top, which a
child would spin by hit-
ting with a whip.

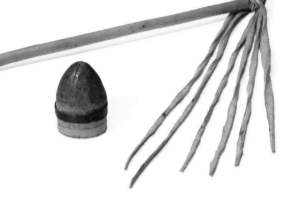

Buffalo Surround (detail)
unknown artist, mid-19th century, collected by Pierre-Jean De Smet
watercolor on paper
Archief Noordbelgische Jezuïetenprovincie, Heverlee, Belgium
CATALOG B/N

Morning and evening speech in buffalo country: *People, remember that when we come to the buffalo country, we are in danger of war at all times. . . . Do not let the enemy get the best of you! All young persons, post yourselves and keep watch!*

33.

Tactique des Chasseurs.

Buffalo Hunting Techniques
Nicolas Point, S.J.
America, ca. 1841–47
ink on paper
4³/₄ x 7³/₈ (12.1 x 18.7)
De Smetiana Collection,
Jesuit Missouri Province
Archives, St. Louis
IX-C9-97

Three methods of killing
bison are seen here:
herding the animals over
a cliff, or "jump"; herding
them into a pound, or
corral; and stalking them
on foot or horseback.

Pierced Shirt
Plateau (Flathead), pre-
1897
Indian tanned leather,
glass seed beads, owl
feathers, cotton
22³/₄ x 44 (57.8 x 111.8)
Field Museum of Natural
History, Chicago 51788

Both Plateau and Black-
feet warriors sometimes
used pierced decoration
on their shirts. This shirt,
collected on the Flathead
Reservation in 1897 along
with a ceremonial head-
dress, was probably worn
on dress occasions. The
owl feathers attached at
both shoulders may refer
to the owner's guardian
spirit.

Bow
Plateau, ca. 1840–50,
collected by Paul Kane
horn, sinew, rawhide
29½ x 6 (75 x 15.4)
Manitoba Museum of Man
and Nature, Winnipeg
H4-5-4

For an experienced hun-
ter, a bow served as well
as a gun. Bows could be
more accurately aimed
and quickly reloaded, and
they were easier to repair,
especially while the
hunter was on horseback.
This bow is made of sec-
tions of mountain-sheep
horn, bent into place and
strung with sinew.

**"Tum-se-ne-ho or
'The Man without
Blood,' Spokan Chief"**
Paul Kane
America, 1847
watercolor on paper
9⅜ x 5½ (23.8 x 14)
Stark Museum of Art,
Orange, Texas 31.78/43,
WWC 43

Tum-se-ne-ho, a Spokane
chief, was painted by
Paul Kane near Fort
Colville on the upper
Columbia River. The chief
wears a pierced shirt
similar to the one col-
lected by George A.
Dorsey in 1897 on the
Flathead Reservation
(left). The bow he carries
may be the one collected
by Paul Kane (below).

Spokan Chief Spokan River

202

War Shirt
Plains (Blackfeet),
ca. 1843
Indian tanned leather,
porcupine quills, hair,
wool, sinew, shell
55 x 63 (139.7 x 160)
Alabama Department of
Archives and History,
Montgomery 86.3147.23

Members of the scientific
Audubon expedition col-
lected this magnificent
Plains shirt at Fort Union
on the upper Missouri
River in 1843. Woman's
Moccasin, a Blackfeet
warrior, gave the shirt to
chief trader Alexander
Culbertson. Ornamenta-
tion consists of scalp
locks and a large quilled
panel. Such a shirt was
imbued with powers that
protected the wearer on
war expeditions.

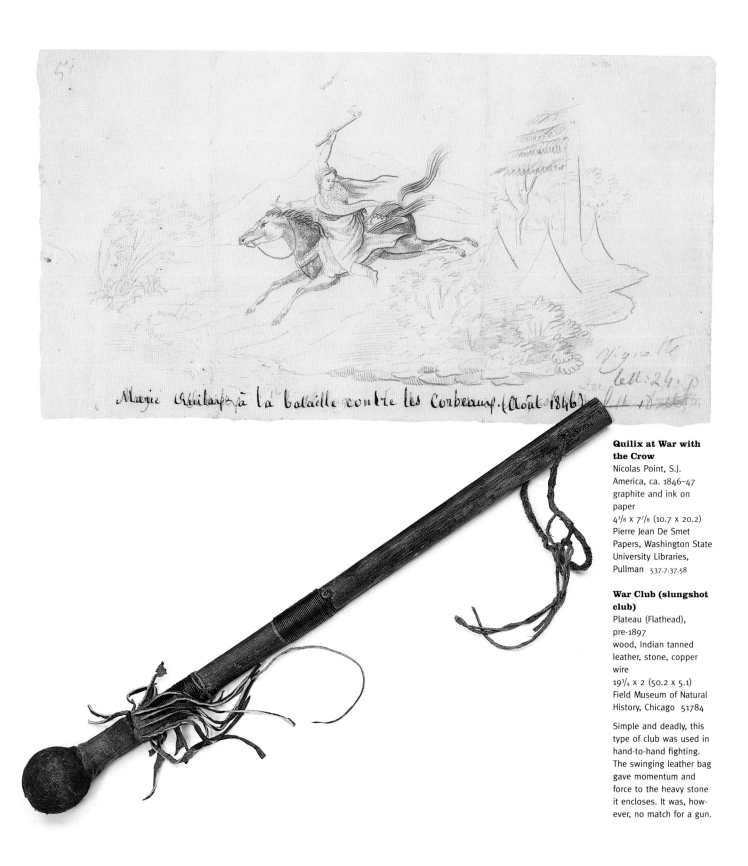

Marquée Culilargée à la bataille contre les Corbeaux. (Août 1846.)

Quilix at War with the Crow
Nicolas Point, S.J.
America, ca. 1846–47
graphite and ink on paper
4³/₈ x 7⁷/₈ (10.7 x 20.2)
Pierre Jean De Smet Papers, Washington State University Libraries, Pullman 537.7.37.58

War Club (slungshot club)
Plateau (Flathead), pre-1897
wood, Indian tanned leather, stone, copper wire
19³/₄ x 2 (50.2 x 5.1)
Field Museum of Natural History, Chicago 51784

Simple and deadly, this type of club was used in hand-to-hand fighting. The swinging leather bag gave momentum and force to the heavy stone it encloses. It was, however, no match for a gun.

Extermination de 30 pieds noirs par les pends d'oreilles
a la tête desquels est une femme nomme Quilix.

**Quilix Leads the
Pend Oreille against
the Blackfeet**
Nicolas Point, S.J.
America, ca. 1841–47
ink on paper
4¹/₂ x 7 (11.4 x 17.8)
De Smetiana Collection,
Jesuit Missouri Province
Archives, St. Louis
IX-C9-69

Women could also go to
war. Quilix, Red Shirt,
was a famed Pend Oreille
woman warrior who led
an attack on the Black-
feet which resulted in the
deaths of thirty enemy
warriors.

Ambrose and Blackfeet on Horse

Ambrose (Shil-che-lum-e-la, Five Crows)
Plateau (Salish),
ca. 1840–47
ink on paper
7¹/₂ x 9¹/₂ (19 x 24.1)
De Smetiana Collection,
Jesuit Missouri Province
Archives, St. Louis
IX-C4-461

During a battle between five hundred lodges of Blackfeet and sixty lodges of Salish and Kalispel, the Salish warrior Ambrose broke his bow. Seeing a Blackfeet with a gun, he pretended to be Blackfeet and called out in that language for the enemy to mount with him on his horse. Ambrose wrestled the Blackfeet's rifle from him and killed him.

War Exploit of Ambrose

Nicolas Point, S.J.
America, ca. 1841–47
ink on paper
4¹/₂ x 7³/₈ (11.4 x 18.7)
De Smetiana Collection,
Jesuit Missouri Province
Archives, St. Louis
IX-C9-73

After watching Ambrose draw his war record and recount his victories, Father Nicolas Point drew his own version of "Ambrose and Blackfeet on Horse" (left). Here Ambrose tricks a Blackfeet into mounting with him on his horse and takes his gun from him. Such a pair of complementary drawings is unparalleled in the art of the early American West.

Ambrose in Blackfeet Fort

Ambrose (Shil-che-lum-e-la, Five Crows)
Plateau (Salish),
ca. 1840–47
ink on paper
9¹/₂ x 7¹/₂ (24.1 x 19)
De Smetiana Collection,
Jesuit Missouri Province
Archives, St. Louis
IX-C4-465

When some Salish came upon a Blackfeet fort, they surrounded it and prepared to destroy the enemy. Ambrose's war medicine allowed him to sneak inside the fort, "count coup," or touch the enemy without killing him, and escape before the Blackfeet fired. Ambrose's drawing of this event shows him with his medicine bag inside the Blackfeet fort.

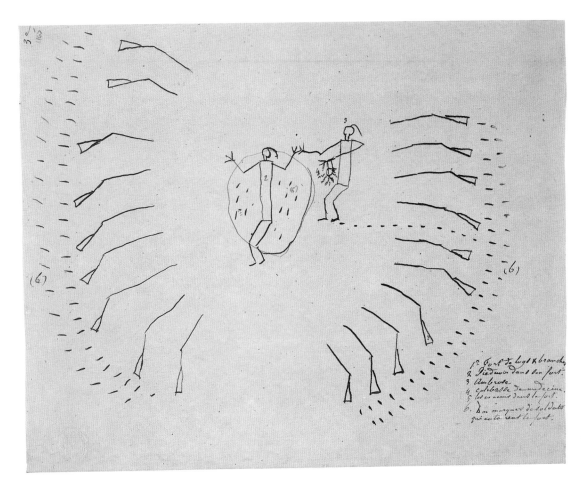

The First to Arrive

Nicolas Point, S.J.
America, ca. 1841–47
ink on paper
4¹/₄ x 6¹/₄ (10.8 x 15.9)
De Smetiana Collection,
Jesuit Missouri Province
Archives, St. Louis
IX-C9-62

Though outnumbered by the better-fortified Black-feet, the Salish had a reputation for bravery in battle. Here, five out-standing Salish war-riors—whose baptismal names were Fidele, Ambrose, Isaac, Ferdi-nand, and Manuel—charge into battle against a much larger enemy force.

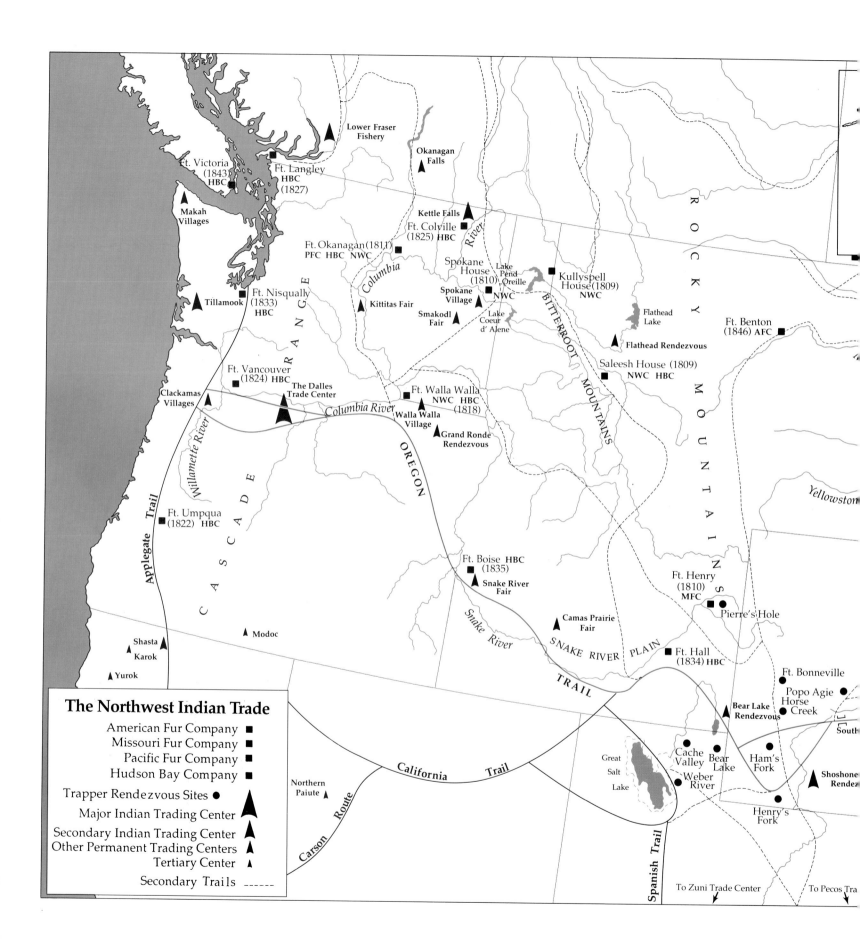

Lower Fraser
Fishery

Okanagan
Falls

Ft. Victoria
(1843)
HBC

Ft. Langley
HBC
(1827)

Makah
Villages

Kettle Falls

Ft. Colville
(1825) HBC

Ft. Okanagan(1811)
PFC HBC NWC

Columbia River

Spokane
House
(1810)

Lake Pend
Oreille

Kullyspell
House(1809)
NWC

Ft. Benton
(1846) AFC

Tillamook

Ft. Nisqually
(1833)
HBC

Kittitas Fair

Spokane
Village
NWC

Smakodl
Fair

Lake
Coeur
d' Alene

Flathead
Lake

Flathead Rendezvous

Saleesh House (1809)
NWC HBC

Ft. Vancouver
(1824) HBC

The Dalles
Trade Center

Clackamas
Villages

Columbia River

Ft. Walla Walla
NWC HBC
(1818)

Walla Walla
Village

Grand Ronde
Rendezvous

OREGON

Willamette River

BITTERROOT MOUNTAINS

ROCKY MOUNTAINS

Yellowstone

Applegate Trail

CASCADE RANGE

Ft. Umpqua
(1822) HBC

Ft. Boise HBC
(1835)

Snake River
Fair

Ft. Henry
(1810)
MFC

Pierre's Hole

Camas Prairie
Fair

Modoc

Snake River

SNAKE RIVER PLAIN

Shasta
Karok

Ft. Hall
(1834) HBC

Ft. Bonneville

Yurok

TRAIL

Popo Agie
Horse
Creek

South

Bear Lake
Rendezvous

The Northwest Indian Trade

American Fur Company ■
Missouri Fur Company ■
Pacific Fur Company ■
Hudson Bay Company ■
Trapper Rendezvous Sites ●
Major Indian Trading Center ▲
Secondary Indian Trading Center ▲
Other Permanent Trading Centers ▲
Tertiary Center ▲

Secondary Trails ------

Northern
Paiute

California   Trail

Great
Salt
Lake

Cache
Valley

Bear
Lake

Ham's
Fork

Weber
River

Shoshone
Rendez

Carson Route

Spanish Trail

To Zuni Trade Center

To Pecos Tra

Henry's
Fork

76

Friendly Trade between the Black-feet and Flathead
Nicolas Point, S.J.
America, ca. 1841–47
ink on paper
4¹/₂ x 7¹/₂ (11.4 x 19.1)
De Smetiana Collection,
Jesuit Missouri Province
Archives, St. Louis
IX-C9-65

49°N

Ft. Union
(1829)
AFC

River

To Mandan →
Hidatsa Trade Centers

To Arikara Trade Center →

vder River

er

ee Crossings

North

Ft. Laramie
(1834) **AFC**

Platte River

0 ——— 200 Miles
    200 Kilometers

Les pieds noirs et les têtes plates font amicalement des échanges mutuels

Flathead

ℊˢ Sohon
May 14ᵗʰ 1854

Ambrose (in baptism) 130305
"Shil-che-lum-e-lä, or "Fire Crows"

A chief of the Flatheads, mentioned many times
in the "Oregon Missions", for his bravery and
generosity.

Portrait of Ambrose
Gustavus Sohon
America, ca. 1855
graphite on paper
10 x 7¼ (25.4 x 18.4)
National Anthropological
Archives, Smithsonian
Institution, Washington,
D.C. 37,416-B

The Salish warrior
Ambrose, also known as
Five Crows, or Shil-che-
lum-e-la, himself drew a
series of pictures based
on his war deeds.

Scotch Cap
Plains (Blackfeet), mid-
19th century
otter or beaver fur, brass
buttons, feathers, thread,
hard leather, wool
9⁵/₈ x 9¼ x 5¼ (24.5 x
23.5 x 13.3)
Department of Anthropol-
ogy, Smithsonian Institu-
tion, Washington, D.C.
7130

Headdresses and head-
gear were important
symbols of rank and
affiliation for Indian
people long before Euro-
pean contact. The fur
trade brought new kinds
of headgear that quickly
became popular. This
visor cap was embel-
lished with feathers and
fur by its Indian owner.
Nicolas Point sketched
many Plateau leaders
wearing visor caps in
the 1840s.

Baldric Pouch with Shoulder Strap

Eastern Woodlands (possibly Ojibwa or Cree), early 19th century
glass seed beads, wool, cotton, silk, sinew
28 x 5⁷/₈ (71.1 x 15)
McCord Museum of Canadian History, Montreal
M189

In the seventeenth century, Ursuline nuns introduced floral motifs to the missionized Huron and Iroquois on the St. Lawrence River. The Huron and Iroquois in turn transmitted these designs to their western neighbors, the Great Lakes Ojibwa and Plains Cree. When the motifs reached the eastern Plateau, native women adapted them in their own way.

North West Company Trade Tokens

England or Canada, 1820
brass, Indian tanned leather
dia. 1¹/₈ (2.9)
Maryhill Museum of Art, Goldendale, Washington
1940.01

Accustomed to a barter system of exchange, native people traded sharply. Fur trade tokens, or "money," such as these disks, seemed useless to them—except as decoration.

"François Lucie, A Cree Half-Breed Guide, 1846"

Paul Kane
Canada, ca. 1847
oil on paper
10⁷/₈ x 8³/₄ (27.7 x 22.3)
Stark Museum of Art, Orange, Texas
31.78/147, POP 9

François Lucie, a Métis of Cree and European descent, is wearing two beaded bandolier bags. Plains and Plateau women made their own versions of such bags, which Indian women farther east had adapted from military shot pouches.

Robert Campbell Coat
Plains (possibly Blackfeet), mid-19th century
Indian tanned leather, porcupine quills, glass pony beads, cotton, sinew, thread, brass, metal and horn buttons, metal hooks and eyes
40¹/₂ x 21 (102.9 x 53.3)
Campbell House Museum, St. Louis 90.603

By the early nineteenth century, Plains Indian women were making European-style clothing using hide, porcupine quills, and beads. Many traders wore fancy frock coats and trousers when they arrived on the Plains and Plateau, and such garments inspired new styles. This beautifully quilled coat was worn by Robert Campbell of St. Louis, a prominent Rocky Mountain fur trader and company owner.

Shot Pouch
Eastern Plains, ca. 1843
loom-woven porcupine quills, bird quills, wool, cotton, silk, sinew, leather, rabbit fur
26¹/₂ x 6⁷/₈ (67.3 x 15.5)
Alabama Department of Archives and History, Montgomery 86.3147.27

After the introduction of firearms, every man on the Plains—Indian, Métis, and white—needed a shot pouch and powder horn. This pouch, collected on the Audubon expedition of 1843, was worn over the shoulder. Its woven quill panels are typical of pouches used by the Red River Métis.

Unstuffed Pad Saddle
Eastern Plains, ca. 1843
Indian tanned leather,
porcupine quills, sinew
20⅛ x 25¼ (51.1 x 64.2)
Alabama Department of
Archives and History,
Montgomery 86.3147.28

Men across the entire
northwestern Plains used
pad saddles stuffed with
soft bison wool. The dia-
mond and rosette motifs
suggest Métis or eastern
Sioux manufacture. Sev-
eral techniques for han-
dling quills were used in
making this saddle.

Free Hunter
Nicholas Point, S.J.
America, ca. 1841
graphite and ink on
paper
3⅛ x 5⅝ (7.9 x 14.3)
Pierre Jean De Smet
Papers, Washington State
University Libraries, Pull-
man 537.7.29.48

By the 1820s, over three
hundred non-Indian men
lived on the Plateau as
independent "free trap-
pers." Many of these
men were Métis, the
sons of fur traders and
their Indian wives. Others
were French-Canadians,
British, and Americans
who had come to the
Plateau as fur trade em-
ployees and then left
their companies.

Crucifix
Northeast (Iroquois), 1776
wood
7⁷/₈ x 2¹/₈ x ³/₄ (20 x
5.4 x 1.9)
Snite Museum of Art, University of Notre Dame,
Indiana 66.31

Iroquois trappers who
had been missionized by
Jesuits in eastern Canada
during the French regime
were already on the Plateau when fur trader and
explorer David Thompson
arrived in 1809. They married Salish women and
introduced an Indianized
version of Christianity. A
Catholic Iroquois carved
this crucifix, dated 1776.

The Plains Across

On the 18th of September [1839] two Catholic Iroquois came to visit us. They had been for twenty-three years among the nation called the Flatheads and Pierced Noses, about a thousand Flemish leagues from where we are. I have never seen any savages so fervent in religion. . . . The sole object of these good Iroquois was to obtain a priest to come and finish what they had so happily commenced. —Father De Smet, Council Bluffs, 1839

"Spokan Garry, 27 May 1855"
Gustavus Sohon
America, ca. 1855
graphite on paper
9 x 7 (22.9 x 17.8)
Washington State Historical Society, Tacoma 61

Spokan Garry and two other Indian boys were sent by the Hudson's Bay Company in 1825 to the Anglican mission school at the Red River Colony (present-day Winnipeg). In 1829, Garry returned to the eastern Plateau with a Bible, an Anglican hymnal, and a rudimentary knowledge of Christianity, which he spread throughout the Plateau. His preachings sparked widespread interest in the new religion and were a catalyst for the search for missionaries.

In 1823 a band of Jesuit novices, including De Smet, and their superiors from White Marsh, Maryland, arrived in the French fur trade community of St. Louis. Burning to become missionaries to the Indians, they opened a Jesuit seminary and a school for Indian boys on a fertile rise of land overlooking the Missouri River. The school failed, and the Jesuits turned instead to the building of St. Louis University and to missions to more remote tribes which, they hoped, had not been corrupted by white influence.

De Smet was ordained in 1827, and by 1839, at age thirty-eight, he was ministering to the Potawatomi Indians at Council Bluffs on the Missouri River. The demoralizing effects of alcohol and white contact on the Potawatomi disillusioned him. It was here that the call of the Rockies came to De Smet as a voice crying from the wilderness.

During the 1830s, four delegations of Salish, Nez Perce, and Iroquois Indians from the Plateau made the hazardous journey across the Great Plains to St. Louis in order to obtain a new spiritual power, or medicine. The first delegation was primarily Nez Perce who, according to tradition, were seeking the "book of heaven," or Bible, which had been shown to them by Spokan Garry, an eastern Plateau youth sent by the Hudson's Bay Company to the Anglican school at present-day Winnipeg during the 1820s. The last three delegations were primarily Salish, accompanied by Catholic Iroquois from the St. Lawrence River who had married among them. A final delegation of two Iroquois found Father De Smet at Council Bluffs in 1839.

The request for Christian missionaries by the Nez Perce and the interior Salish-speaking tribes has perplexed historians for nearly a century. The tribes themselves have different explanations today. Those missionized by the Protestants in the 1830s and 1840s claim they were looking for Christian teachers of the Bible; tribes missionized by the Jesuits believe their ancestors called specifically for Black Robes.

Both explanations derive from Indian prophecies, recorded as early as 1841, of the coming of white men from the east who had access to a supernatural power which protected them from disease and could bring the dead to life. Some Plateau tribes actively sought this power, even at the risk of the apocalyptic destruction hinted at by their prophets. The explanations also derive from the influence of other Indians, such as Spokan Garry among the Nez Perce, and Iroquois trappers from Quebec among the Salish, who variously introduced Protestant or Catholic ideas, symbols, and rituals prior to the missionaries' arrival.

In 1840, with one of the two Iroquois delegates as a guide, De Smet made an exploratory trip to the Rocky Mountains to visit the Salish. He returned to St. Louis to seek funds and priests, and in the summer of 1841 he once more headed west. He was accompanied by two other Jesuit priests, Nicolas Point, a French educator and architect, and Gregory Mengarini, a Roman linguist and musician; three Jesuit lay brothers who were all craftsmen; and six French-Canadian trappers. At Westport (present-day Kansas City), the Jesuits joined the first overland wagon train bound for California—the Bidwell-Bartleson party of sixty-nine men, women, and children.

Lacking their own expedition leader, the settlers relied on De Smet's experienced guide, Thomas Fitzpatrick, and his assistant, the famed Iroquois hunter and guide Ignace Hatchiorau-quacha, also known as John Grey. Together the two parties crossed the Plains and Rockies along a route that within a decade would bring tens of thousands of white settlers into the West. After three long months on the trail, the group split up at Soda Springs in present-day Idaho, the missionaries heading north toward the main camp of the Salish, where they arrived on August 15, 1941, the Feast of the Assumption.

The Dream of a New Paraguay As the Jesuit missionaries crossed the great sea of prairie grass and desert sagebrush of western North America, they dreamed. In the evenings, by camp light, they read scripture and a book by L. V. Muratori describing the legendary seventeenth-century Jesuit Reductions among the Guaraní Indians of Paraguay. Even before they arrived at the main Salish camp, De Smet and Point were envisioning a new Paraguay. Remotely situated and isolated from contaminating white influences, the peaceful Salish seemed a chosen people. Nicolas Point drafted architectural plans for the first reduction, complete with row houses and fields fanning out in a crescent around a wilderness cathedral (see p. 92).

MISSIONARY INTELLIGENCE.

HEAR ! HEAR !

Who will respond to the call from beyond the Rocky Mountains?

Messrs. Editors :—The communication of brother G. P. Disosway, including one from the Wyandot agent, on the subject of the deputation of the Flat-head Indians to Gen. Clarke, has excited in many in this section intense interest. And to be short about it, we are for having a mission established there at once. I have proposed the following plan :—Let two suitable men, unencumbered with families, and possessing the spirit of martyrs, throw themselves into the nation. Live with them—learn their language—preach Christ to them—and, as the way opens, introduce schools,

De Smet's Cassock
America, mid-19th century
wool, cotton
55½ x 49½ (141 x 125.7)
Museum of the Western Jesuit Missions, Florissant, Missouri   991.47

De Smet liked Indians, and the feeling seems to have been mutual. Physically strong and brave, he enjoyed wilderness travel. He rode an estimated 200,000 miles on horseback in his lifetime.

De Smet was open, honest, and generous, traits that Indian people valued. That De Smet knew the Great Prayer—the Catholic Mass—made him irresistible. No symbol of De Smet was more powerful than his cassock. In the minds of many Indian tribes, and especially the Sioux, he *was* Black Robe.

"Missionary Intelligence: Hear! Hear!"
article by W. Fisk, *Christian Advocate and Journal and Zion's Herald*, March 22, 1833
American Antiquarian Society, Worcester, Massachusetts

The arrival in St. Louis of the first Indian delegation from the Northern Rockies created a stir in the eastern Protestant press. In response to the clarion call for missionaries, Presbyterians Marcus and Narcissa Whitman, Henry and Eliza Spalding, and John Gray headed to the Northern Rockies in 1837. Protestant missions to the Nez Perce, Cayuse, and Spokane tribes were soon established.

84

St. Louis Cathedral, 1840
J. C. Wild
America, ca. 1840
lithograph
Missouri Historical Society, St. Louis PB 912

When De Smet arrived in St. Louis in 1823, its Catholic cathedral was a nondescript brick building. Under Bishop Rosati, the cornerstone for a new cathedral on the waterfront was laid in 1831, and Mass was first celebrated in 1835.

Departure from Westport

Nicolas Point, S.J.
America, ca. 1841
graphite and ink on paper
$3\frac{1}{2} \times 5\frac{7}{8}$ (8.8 x 15)
Pierre Jean De Smet
Papers, Washington State
University Libraries,
Pullman 537.7.1.1

The six Jesuits left Westport, Missouri, on April 30, 1841. As the staging ground for wagon traffic across the Oregon Trail, Westport at that time housed twenty-three families, mainly retired Iroquois and French Canadian trappers and their native wives. Nicolas Point built the chapel shown here in November 1840.

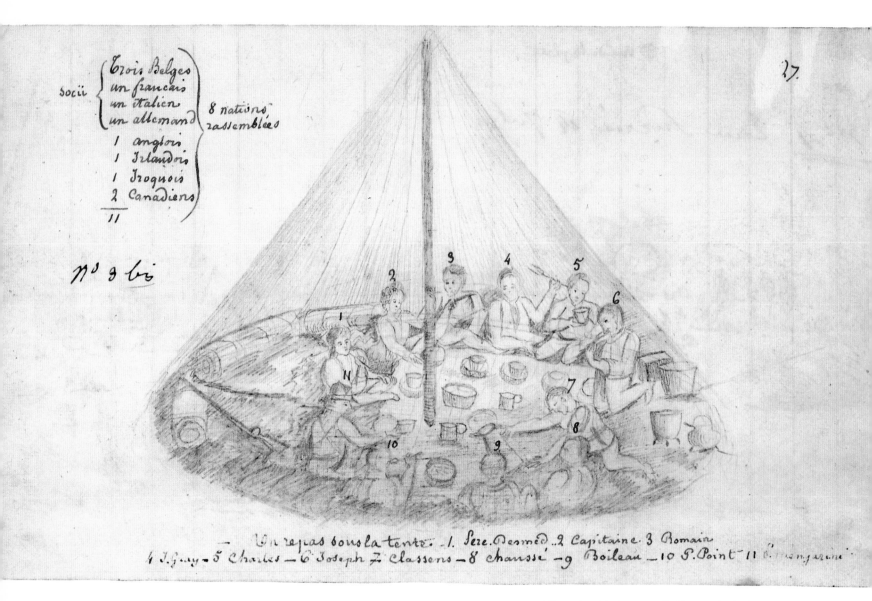

socii
{
Trois Belges
un français
un italien
un allemand
} 8 nations rassemblées
1 anglais
1 Irlandois
1 Iroquois
2 Canadiens
—
11

N° 9 bis

— Un repas sous la tente. 1. Père Desméd 2 Capitaine. 3 Romain 4 J. Guy — 5 Charles — 6 Joseph 7 Classens — 8 chaussé — 9 Boileau — 10 P. Point 11 Mengarini

Dinner in a Tent
Nicolas Point, S.J.
America, ca. 1841
graphite and ink on paper
3½ x 6 (8.9 x 15.2)
Pierre Jean De Smet
Papers, Washington State
University Libraries,
Pullman 537.7.12.23

The European Jesuits chosen for the Rocky Mountain mission brought varied backgrounds and skills to wilderness work. Gregory Mengarini was a skilled linguist, musician, and physician; Nicolas Point an architect, artist, and educator; William Claessens, a blacksmith; Charles Huet, a carpenter; and Joseph Specht, a tinsmith and laborer. Here they share dinner on the trail.

John Grey, Iroquois

Nicolas Point, S.J.
America, ca. 1841
graphite and ink on paper
3 1/8 x 5 7/8 (7.9 x 14.9)
Pierre Jean De Smet
Papers, Washington State
University Libraries,
Pullman 537.7.28.46

Ignace Hatchiorauquacha,
also known as John Grey,
was a famous Iroquois
hunter and guide who
had settled with several
other Iroquois and their
families at Westport in
1832. The missionaries'
guide, Thomas Fitzpatrick,
enlisted him to assist in
leading the Jesuits west-
ward.

Member of the
Jesuit Party

Nicolas Point, S.J.
America, ca. 1841
graphite on paper
3 1/2 x 5 5/8 (8.9 x 14.3)
Pierre Jean De Smet
Papers, Washington State
University Libraries,
Pullman 537.4.9

This fine portrait of an
unidentified member of
the De Smet party might
portray a Jesuit or one of
the six French-Canadian
trappers who accompa-
nied them. Even the mis-
sionaries wore ordinary
clothes on the trek, but
because of an attack by
hostile Bannock Indians,
Mengarini persuaded
De Smet to put on his
cassock.

Portrait of an
Unidentified Indian
Woman

Nicolas Point, S.J.
America, ca. 1841
graphite on paper
2 7/8 x 5 1/8 (7.3 x 13)
Pierre Jean De Smet
Papers, Washington State
University Libraries,
Pullman 537.4.9

This rare portrait of an
Indian woman drawn by
Nicolas Point may be of
Marianne Neketichou, the
wife of Ignace Hatchior-
auquacha, or John Grey.
She was the only Indian
woman known to have
accompanied the mission-
ary party.

Sleeping Traveler

Nicolas Point, S.J.
America, ca. 1841
graphite and ink
on paper
3 x 5 1/2 (7.6 x 14)
De Smetiana Collection,
Jesuit Missouri Province
Archives, St. Louis
IX-C9-29a

Believed to be a portrait
of Gregory Mengarini,
this sketch captures the
exhaustion after a day's
travel in the wagon train
and the rigors of the
Jesuits' new life.

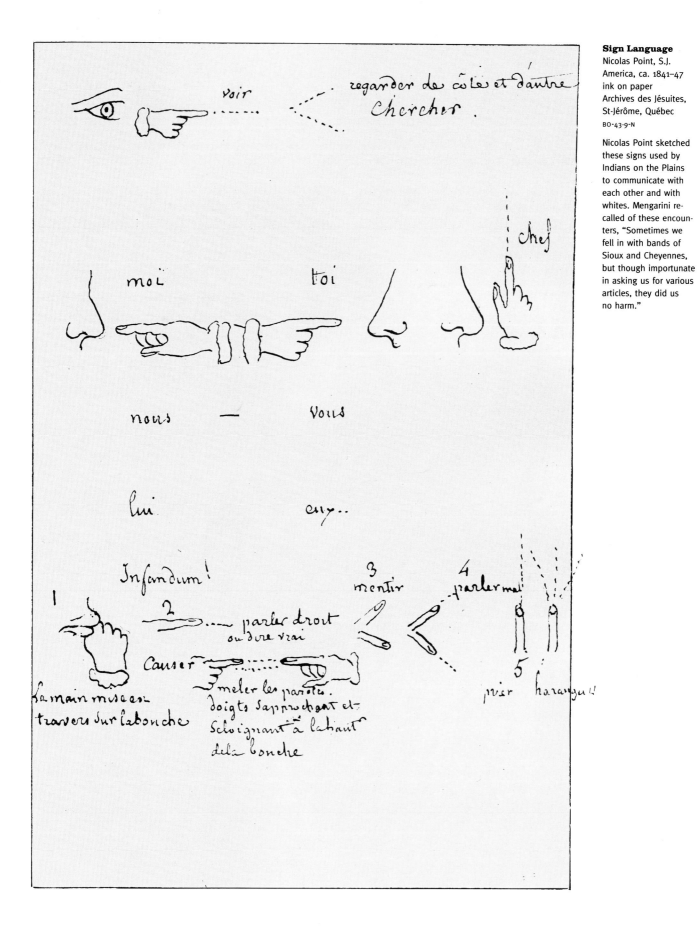

voir

regarder de côte et d'autre
Chercher.

moi   toi   chef

nous — vous

lui   eux..

Infandum!
3 mentir
4 parler mal

1
2 ..... parler droit
ou dire vrai

Causer

5
pour haranguer!

La main mise en travers sur la bouche

mêler les paroles. doigts s'approchant et s'éloignant à l'haut de la bouche

Sign Language
Nicolas Point, S.J.
America, ca. 1841–47
ink on paper
Archives des Jésuites,
St-Jérôme, Québec
BO-43-9-N

Nicolas Point sketched
these signs used by
Indians on the Plains
to communicate with
each other and with
whites. Mengarini re-
called of these encoun-
ters, "Sometimes we
fell in with bands of
Sioux and Cheyennes,
but though importunate
in asking us for various
articles, they did us
no harm."

Tule Lodge
Nicolas Point, S.J.
America, ca. 1841
graphite on paper
4½ x 7 (11.4 x 17.8)
De Smetiana Collection,
Jesuit Missouri Province
Archives, St. Louis
IX-C9-34

This undated drawing
of the interior of a tule
mat lodge occupied by
the Jesuits illustrates the
missionaries' initial de-
pendence upon Indian
generosity for essential
shelter and food. Jesuit
Brother William Claessens
would later refer to the
early months among the
Salish as the best times
of "our mounten live."

Chimney Rock
Nicolas Point, S.J.
America, ca. 1841
graphite on paper
3 x 6 (7.6 x 15.2)
Pierre Jean De Smet
Papers, Washington State
University Libraries,
Pullman 537.7.7.12

This famous landmark,
located in the northwest-
ern corner of the present
state of Nebraska, sig-
naled to all travelers on
the Oregon Trail that
they were headed on the
right road toward Fort
Laramie, near the head-
waters of the Platte
River. Once past Chimney
Rock, travelers entered
the high Plains.

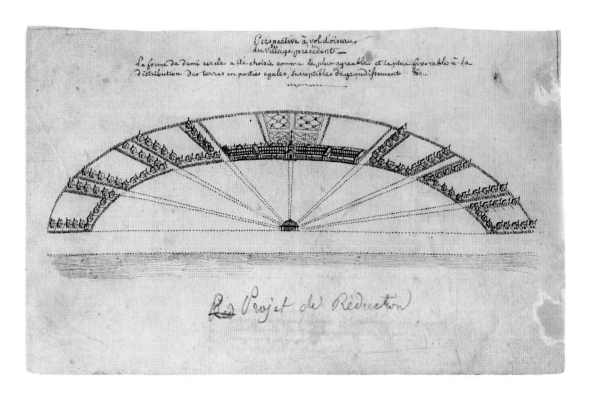

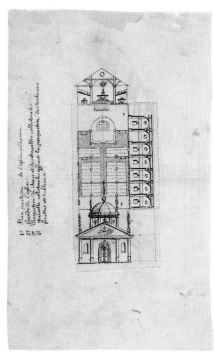

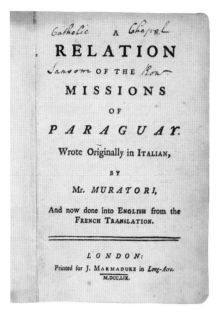

De Smet called Muratori's *Relation* the missionaries' *vade mecum,* or reference manual. The title page of the first English edition is reproduced here. Although the *Relation* was first printed in Italian, it is likely that the party of Flemish, French, Italian, and Swiss Jesuits carried either the French or English edition with them on their overland journey in 1841.

Ste. Marie Village des Têtes-Plates.
St. Mary's among the Flat Heads.

23

Early Northwest Missions, 1837–42

49°N

Tshimakain, 1838
ABCFM

Flathead
Lake

Columbia River

Lake
Coeur d' Alene

Sacred Heart Mission
(St. Joseph) to the Coeur d' Alene
RC

St. Joe River

Bitterroot River

Nisqually, 1839
M

Snake River

St. Mary's
Mission
to the
Flathead
RC

Waailatpu, 1836
ABCFM

Lapwai, 1836
ABCFM

Clatsop
M   1840

Columbia River

Kamiah, 1838
ABCFM

St. Paul's
Mission
on the
Willamette
RC

Salmon   River

Willamette, 1835
M

Willamette River

C A S C A D E   R A N G E

Snake

River

Roman Catholic   RC

American Board of Commissioners
for Foreign Missions   ABCFM

Methodist   M

0   100 Miles
          100 Kilometers

Jesuit Missions in the Northwest in 1847

St. Joseph Mission
to the
Okanagan

Station of the
Immaculate Heart of Mary
among the
Kootenais

St. Paul Mission
to the
Colville

49°N

St. Francis Regis Mission
to the Cree

Station of the Assumption
among the Arcs à Plats

St. Ignatius Mission
to the Kalispel

Sacred Heart Mission
("Old Mission")
to the
Coeur d' Alene

Flathead
Lake

Columbia River

Lake
Coeur d' Alene

St. Francis Borgia
Mission to the
Upper Pend Oreille

St. Joe River

Bitterroot

Snake River

St. Mary's Mission
to the
Flathead

River

Columbia River

Salmon

River

Willamette River

St. Francis Xavier

C A S C A D E   R A N G E

Snake River

0   100 Miles
        100 Kilometers

SION LAUDA SALVATOREM.

Procession of the Blessed Sacrament
Nicolas Point, S.J.
America, ca. 1841–46
oil on paper
4¹/₂ x 7¹/₂ (11.5 x 19)
Archives des Jésuites,
St-Jérôme, Québec

BO-43-14

Religious processions and feast day celebrations engaged the entire community in ritual drama. This painting illustrates the procession at St. Mary's on the Feast of Corpus Christi in 1842. For the feast day, Nicolas Point made a monstrance to hold the consecrated wafer, which the missionaries taught the Salish to worship as Christ's actual body.

Wilderness Kingdom

This tymes where the best of our mounten live. We where lyk in heaven. —Brother William Claessens, ca. 1885

The missionaries' first years among the Salish and Coeur d'Alene were the stuff of fables. De Smet wrote in astonishment of devoted Indians who gathered from dawn to dusk to hear

Altar in a Tipi
Nicolas Point, S.J.
America, ca. 1841–47
watercolor on paper
4 x 6¹/₂ (10.2 x 15.9)
De Smetiana Collection,
Jesuit Missouri Province
Archives, St. Louis
IX-C9-35

This watercolor of a Catholic altar in an Indian tule mat lodge, the traditional housing of Plateau Indian people, eloquently expresses the hopes of the missionary artist Nicolas Point for the conversion of the Northwest tribes. At the same time, it evokes the possibility of a merging of Christianity with Salish beliefs.

the Jesuits recite the Great Prayer, learn their catechism, and sing European hymns. In October 1841, he observed, "The nation of the Flatheads appear to be a chosen people—'the elect of God.' . . . It would be easy to make this tribe a model for other tribes—the seed of 200,000 Christians, who would be as fervent as were the converted Indians of Paraguay. Among them, dissensions, quarrels, injuries, and enmities are unknown."

St. Mary's, the first of a dozen Jesuit missions and stations established among the Plateau tribes between 1841 and 1846, was situated in the Bitterroot valley of northwestern Montana, whose broad, well-watered plain and mild climate seemed perfectly suited for a reduction supported by agriculture. The Flathead, like their Coeur d'Alene neighbors, wanted the healing powers of the Catholic sacraments which the Jesuits described as "medicines of the soul," but they expressed little interest in farming, preferring the variety and dependability of roots, waterfowl, fish, bison, and deer.

Nicolas Point had dreamed of building a cathedral in the wilderness, but he celebrated midnight mass at the new Sacred Heart mission to the Coeur d'Alene at Christmas 1842 in a shelter of saplings and bark. Although Father Point said the Coeur d'Alene gave their hearts to Jesus that night, meeting the new God, the Mother of God, and God's son inside a man-made dwelling must have seemed strange to the Indians. For the Coeur d'Alene, the sacred was all around them—in the trees, lakes, and mountains.

Conversion is not a simple matter. The Salish and Coeur d'Alene naturally saw Christianity through Indian eyes, and the Jesuits were aware of this. As Point confided: "To those who would blame a Catholic missionary for going along with the Indians in these circumstances, we would answer: with the Indians particularly, 'tis better to graft than to fell."

The Jesuits were innovative and sophisticated educators. They taught in the native languages. They used aural and visual aids such as pictures, charts, music, and drama. They staged contests and "catechism bees," and rewarded the winners with prizes. And they asked Indian leaders to help them in their work by serving as Christian models and mentors.

The Salish and Coeur d'Alene, however, did not abandon their traditions when they became Christians. Like European glass beads sewn to buckskin clothing, Christianity added to, but did not replace, Indian ways of thinking about the sacred. Jesus and the saints were new guardian spirits; Christian hymns were new medicine songs that could protect and heal; and the sacraments were powerful new medicines. "Generally speaking," Gregory Mengarini recalled in a memoir, "the prayers of our Indians consisted in asking to live a long time, to kill plenty of animals and enemies, and to steal the greatest number of horses possible."

Conversion or Convergence? Two different worlds met at the Rocky Mountain missions in 1841–42. De Smet believed he had been called to found a wilderness kingdom, in which Indian hunters would gradually be transformed into peaceful Christian farmers. Although the Salish had asked for the power of the Christian God to strengthen their lives as Indians, they did not expect to live like whites. Indian people saw similarities between Catholicism and native religion, but many points did not match at all. The Salish lacked a concept of sin, and did not understand why a loving God would send his children to hell. Nor did they at first understand the appeal of heaven, since there were no relatives or buffalo there. Their hopes that Christian power would bring them success in hunting and in war eventually brought conflict with the priests, who wanted them to stay at home and farm.

The Jesuits tried to end the constant battles between the Salish and the Blackfeet by establishing a mission to the Blackfeet. The Salish felt betrayed. Christian medicine power brought them victory in war; now the Black Robes were sharing the power with their enemies. At the same time, the missionaries stopped accompanying the Salish on the hunt, and many of the Salish began to return to their old medicines.

After 1846, Victor, the principal chief of the Bitterroot Salish and a friend of the Jesuits, could not get his people to listen to the missionaries or to protect the mission against continuing Blackfeet raids. Finally, in 1850, the Jesuits closed the mission and sold their buildings and farm to Major John Owen, a local trader. St. Mary's mission to the Salish did not reopen until 1866.

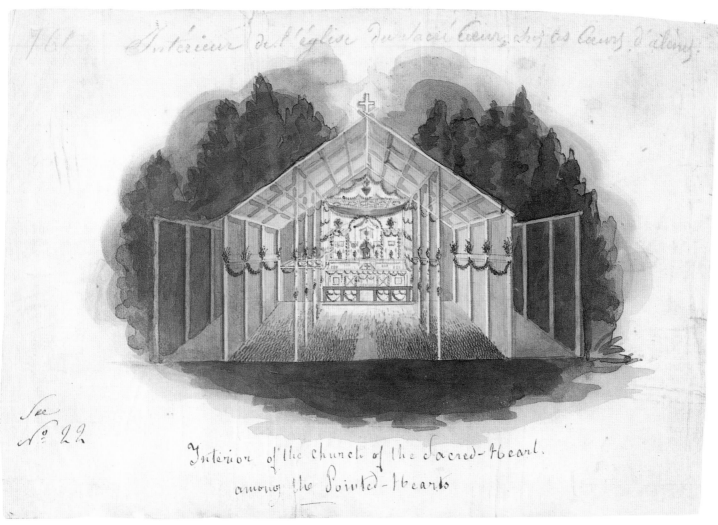

Sacred Heart Mission to the Coeur d'Alene, Christmas, 1842
Nicolas Point, S.J.
America, 1842
watercolor on paper
4⅝ x 6⅝ (11.7 x 16.8)
Pierre Jean De Smet Papers, Washington State University Libraries, Pullman 537.7.51.73

Es tsw ḥél-ku-pee tel ku-kú-sem
Łu ku-túnt il-i-mée-hum
L kam-pee-lé e-mú-tee.
Sku-quée-melt łu Yay-su Klee

He is coming down from the star
The great Chief
With us he is living
The infant Jesus Christ
—Salish hymn

A little before midnight the firing of muskets announced that the church had just been opened. Waves of worshipers hurried toward the palace of the Infant God and, at the sight of the night suddenly changed into splendid day, they were moved to cry, "Jesus, I give you my heart." —Nicolas Point, S.J., Christmas, 1842

Eemotesoglem ou le Boeuf des Montagnes.
Pierre Ignace

Quatre nicht She l'homme qui marche sur sa couverte
Paulin

Tskilkskwe.
Damas

Chiefs of the Coeur d'Alene When Sacred Heart, the Second Rocky Mountain Mission, Was Founded in 1842

Nicolas Point, S.J.
America, ca. 1842
ink on paper
8⅝ x 5⅞ (22 x 15)
Archives des Jésuites,
St-Jérôme, Québec
BO-43-15

Although the Coeur d'Alene were reputedly unfriendly to whites, their chiefs welcomed Father De Smet in 1841 with such enthusiasm that the Jesuits established the second reduction among this "small but interesting tribe." Sacred Heart was to prove the most enduring mission established by De Smet.

Eemotesoglem (Pierre Ignace)

Nicolas Point, S.J.
America, ca. 1842
graphite on paper
7¼ x 4¾ (18.4 x 12.1)
De Smetiana Collection,
Jesuit Missouri Province
Archives, St. Louis
IX-C9-12

Eemotesoglem, or Sitting Bull, was subchief of the Spokane valley bands of Coeur d'Alene. Known as an orator, storyteller, and leader of communal deer hunts, he died and was buried at Cataldo mission in 1854 at the age of eighty.

Paulin

Nicolas Point, S.J.
America, ca. 1842
graphite on paper
7¼ x 4¾ (18.4 x 12.1)
De Smetiana Collection,
Jesuit Missouri Province
Archives, St. Louis
IX-C9-9

Paulin's band occupied a secluded valley at the foot of Cataldo Mountain along the Coeur d'Alene River. Jesuits selected this site in 1846 for the new mission of the Sacred Heart after flooding at the St. Joseph River site forced a relocation.

Tskilkskwe (Damas)

Nicolas Point, S.J.
America, ca. 1842
graphite on paper
7¼ x 4¾ (18.4 x 12.1)
De Smetiana Collection,
Jesuit Missouri Province
Archives, St. Louis
IX-C9-11

Tskilkskwe, or Five Names, was the elder son of Gabriel, the chief of the St. Joseph River band of Coeur d'Alene, among whom the first Sacred Heart mission was located.

Insula (Michel)
Nicolas Point, S.J.
America, ca. 1841–42
graphite on paper
7¼ x 4¾ (18.4 x 12.1)
De Smetiana Collection,
Jesuit Missouri Province
Archives, St. Louis
IX-C9-7

Both a preliminary sketch
and a finished portrait
survive of Insula, also
known as Red Feather
and the Little Chief, who
was baptized Michel
after the archangel of war.
A highly regarded Flat-
head leader and accom-
plished warrior, Insula
adopted as brothers the
American fur traders Rob-
ert Campbell and Thomas
Fitzpatrick. Brave, loyal,
and trustworthy, Insula
embodied the virtues of
his people that so im-
pressed the Jesuits.

Victor
Nicolas Point, S.J.
America, ca. 1841–42
graphite on paper
Pierre Van de Velde,
Moortsele, Belgium

Victor, son and succes-
sor to Big Face, who wel-
comed De Smet at Pierre's
Hole in 1840, was princi-
pal chief of the Bitterroot
Salish until his death in
1870.

**Chiefs of the Flathead
When St. Mary's, the
First Rocky Mountain
Mission, Was
Founded in 1841**
Nicolas Point, S.J.
America, ca. 1841
ink on paper
9¹¹/₁₆ x 6¹¹/₁₆ (24.7 x 17)
Archives des Jésuites,
St-Jérôme, Québec
BO-43-15

Interior of St. Mary's Church, Flat-Head Mission. Communion

asten. See letter the 4th

Interior of St. Mary's Church Flathead Mission: Communion at Easter

Nicolas Point, S.J.
America, 1842
watercolor on paper
4½ x 6⅝ (11.4 x 16.8)
De Smetiana Collection,
Jesuit Missouri Province
Archives, St. Louis
IX-C9-6

This sketch of first communion at St. Mary's in 1842 evokes the tender, intense mood of the early Rocky Mountain missions. The Salish made many of the chapel decorations, including the woven rush mats covering the floor and ceiling and the cedar garlands, while the Jesuits contributed the pictures of the Virgin, the Sacred Heart of Jesus, and the Stations of the Cross.

The Miraculous Medal

France, ca. 1830–80
metal
⅞ x ½ (2.2 x 1.3)
Montana Historical Society, Gift of Susan R. Near,
Helena 84.29.02

Both Jesuits and Indians believed that sacred objects possessed the power to heal and protect. The Miraculous Medal, struck after apparitions of Mary appeared in France in 1830, was worn close to the heart—just as tokens of guardian spirits were sewn by Indian people to their clothes. Father Mengarini said that the Salish placed such importance on medals like this that "when they are lost even grown men cry in sorrow."

10

Nº 1.

1844

Consécration des armes _____ avant le départ pour la chasse

Tous les jours deux fois les chasseurs ont invoqué le sacré cœur et la sainte vierge pour se rendre le ciel propice en tout.
Ils ont prié S. Michel pour être fort contre leurs ennemis, S. Raphaël pour qu'il les protège dans la route.
S. Hubert pour faire une bonne chasse, et depuis la neuvaine de S. François xavier, l'apôtre des Indes
pour la conversion des Idolâtres on verra quaucune espèce de secours ne leur a manqué

Blessing of the Arms before Leaving for the Hunt
Nicolas Point, S.J.
America, 1844
watercolor on paper
4⅞ x 6¾ (12.5 x 17.2)
De Smetiana Collection,
Jesuit Missouri Province
Archives, St. Louis
IX-C9-82

Medecine d'Ignace

Ignace's Medicine Power

Nicolas Point, S.J.
America, ca. 1842
ink on paper
4¼ x 6⅞ (10.8 x 17.5)
De Smetiana Collection,
Jesuit Missouri Province
Archives, St. Louis
IX-C9-18

These two pictures vividly portray one of the similarities between Salish and Catholic beliefs. Above, Ignace, a Coeur d'Alene chief, goes to the mountains to sweat, fast, and pray for a guardian animal spirit to give him powerful hunting medicines. On the facing page, Salish warriors leaving for the winter buffalo hunt ask for the protection of St. Michael, St. Raphael, and St. Hubert. Point said the Salish chose these three saints as their patrons because they aided warriors, travelers, and hunters.

Notice the male deer at the left of center in both pictures. In "Ignace's Medicine Power," the deer, a guardian animal spirit, bestows powerful hunting medicines on Ignace. In "Blessing of the Arms," Salish hunters are blessed by St. Hubert, the Catholic patron of hunters whose symbol is a stag with a cross between its antlers.

A Battle on the Plains with the Blackfeet
Nicolas Point, S.J.
America, ca. 1841–46
graphite on paper
4¼ x 7 (10.8 x 17.8)
De Smetiana Collection,
Jesuit Missouri Province
Archives, St. Louis
IX-C9-61

Just as they had relied
on their war medicine to
help them in battle, Salish
converts believed in the
powers of Jesus and Mary
to protect them against
their enemies. Here, prayers to the Immaculate
Heart of Mary were an-
swered by a Salish victory
over the Blackfeet.

Un chef pied noir après avoir vu l'échelle catholique que lui explique Ambrose chef Tête-plate demande à être incorporé à la peuplade des Têtes-plates, lui et ses vingt-huit loges

Ambrose Instructs a Blackfeet Chief with the Ladder
Nicolas Point, S.J.
America, ca. 1841–47
ink on paper
4¼ x 6⅝ (10.8 x 16.8)
De Smetiana Collection, Jesuit Missouri Province Archives, St. Louis
IX-C9-67

The Small Robes were the only band of Blackfeet friendly to the Salish. After learning about the Jesuit God from Ambrose, their leader asked that his band of twenty-eight lodges be allowed to live among the Salish so that they could learn the Great Prayer. A short while later, the Small Robes were virtually wiped out in a battle with the Crow.

The Art of Conversion
Nicolas Point, S.J.
America, ca. 1841–46
oil on paper
3¹⁵⁄₁₆ x 6¹⁄₁₆ (10 x 15.5)
Archives des Jésuites, St-Jérôme, Québec
BO43-14

"I made a great effort to speak to them through pictures. . . . Some scenes showed the mysteries; others, the sacraments. . . . This method of instruction had two noticeable advantages. While the truths entered their souls through the eyes, the great virtues were infused into their hearts"—Nicolas Point, S.J., ca. 1855

Sodality Sash

America, 19th century
woven textile, metal lace,
thread
96¹/₂ x 5⁵/₈ (245.1 x 14.3)
Oregon Province of the
Society of Jesus, Portland
SJ 323

Male members of reli-
gious associations called
sodalities wore sashes
like this on feast days
such as Corpus Christi.
Such associations pro-
vided new roles for lead-
ers and their families
who converted to Chris-
tianity. At St. Mary's,
Father De Smet named
Chief Vincent and his
wife, Agnes, as heads
of the Society of the Sa-
cred Heart of Jesus and
the Society of the Im-
maculate Heart of Mary.

**Lord's Prayer in the
Flathead Language**

Salish transcription by
Gregory Mengarini, S.J.,
ca. 1841–46
ink on paper
9¹/₈ x 11¹/₈ (23.2 x 28.3)
De Smetiana Collection,
Jesuit Missouri Province
Archives, St. Louis
IX-C7

Father Mengarini, a
skilled linguist, compiled
the first Salish grammar
and vocabulary. He also
translated the catechism,
the Lord's Prayer, the
Credo, the Litany, and
other prayers and hymns
from Latin for Indian use
at the Salish and Coeur
d'Alene missions.

JESUS CHRIST

**The Protestant Chart
or Ladder**
Eliza Spalding
Northwest America,
ca. 1842
ink, berry dyes, natural
pigment on paper
67¹¹/₁₆ x 21¹³/₁₆
(172 x 55.5)
Oregon Historical Society,
Portland 87847-C

The Catholic Ladder

Paris, 1843
lithograph, ink autograph
of Pierre-Jean De Smet, S.J.
25 x 9⁷/₈ (63.5 x 25)
Jozef Dauwe, Lebbeke,
Belgium

Catholic and Protestant
missionaries bitterly
fought each other to save
Indian souls. Each group
thought the other was
damned, as these teaching
charts show. The Catholic
ladder, invented by Bishop
Blanchet in Oregon in 1838
and revised by De Smet
in 1843, shows the Protestants marooned on a dead
end branch of the one true
road to salvation.

The Protestant ladder,
created by Eliza Spalding,
wife of the Reverend
Henry Spalding, first
Presbyterian missionary
to the Nez Perce, pictures
two roads leading from the
Garden of Eden. The Prot-
estants are on the straight
and narrow path leading
to heaven. The Catholics
are on the wrong road,
and the pope is falling
into the fires of hell on
Judgment Day.

This warfare between
Christian missionaries con-
fused the Indians, who had
been taught that they were
all children of the same
God.

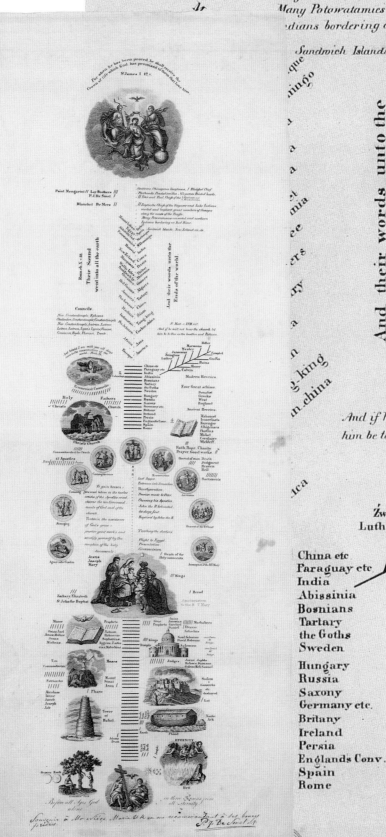

Diverse Clothing and Animals
unknown Indian artist,
ca. 1846–47, collected
by Nicolas Point, S.J.
pastel on paper
10³/₁₆ x 5⁷/₈ (26 x 1.5)
Archives des Jésuites,
St-Jérôme, Québec
BO-43-14

Stock animals were a nov-
elty for Indian males, but
the sedentary lifestyle they
represented contrasted
with the free-ranging life
of the hunt. An anonymous
Indian artist, near Fort
Benton on the upper Mis-
souri River, captured the
differences with sharp and
humorous detail.

The Trade and Distribution of Liquor, Etc.
unknown Indian artist, ca. 1846–47, collected by Nicolas Point, S.J. pastel on paper 8³/₁₆ x 5⁷/₈ (20.8 x 15) Archives des Jésuites, St-Jérôme, Québec BO-43-14

Prior to contact with whites, mind-altering or hallucinogenic substances, including caffeine, were unknown to Plateau and Plains tribes. The powerful, even "electrifying" effects of alcohol were vividly portrayed by an unknown Indian near Fort Benton in this drawing, which suggests that intoxication may have been viewed initially as a form of spiritual possession.

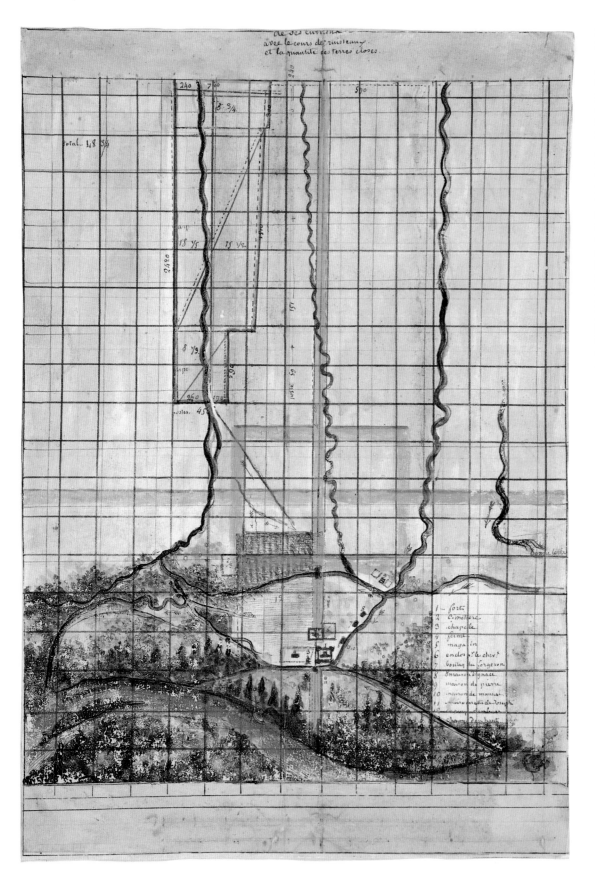

Plan of St. Mary's Mission

Nicolas Point, S.J.
America, ca. 1841–42
watercolor on paper
9 x 6¹/₁₆ (23 x 15.5)
Archives des Jésuites,
St-Jérôme, Québec
BO-43-14

At St. Mary's mission,
Point designed a village
"built in the quadrangu-
lar shape of a fortress."
The houses, spaced fifty
feet from one another,
were surrounded by
"a lawn of sixty feet
square." But the open
location and size made
the village vulnerable
to Blackfeet attack. The
plan was based on a
European rather than a
Salish way of living on
the land and reflected
a lack of understanding
of Salish concerns.

Worshiping False Idols

Nicolas Point, S.J.
America, ca. 1842–46
ink on paper
4½ x 7 (11.4 x 17.8)
De Smetiana Collection,
Jesuit Missouri Province
Archives, St. Louis
IX-C9-22

The Jesuits half-heartedly tolerated the grafting of Christianity onto Indian religious beliefs in order to win converts. At the same time, they attempted to discredit their rivals, the medicine men, and to put a stop to Indian religious ceremonies, saying they were evil and the work of the devil. Priests told converts to throw away their medicine bags, and many did.

Idoles foulées aux pieds au sommet du Smatiokann.

Skull and Crossbones

Anthony Ravalli, S.J.
America, ca. 1860–80
wood, paint
6½ x 10½ x 5¼
(16.5 x 26.7 x 13.3)
Montana Historical
Society, Gift of the St.
Ignatius Mission, Helena
X04.01.02

This carving represents Jesus' death. Indian people thought that those who did wrong in this life would be punished in this life: they would get sick, have bad luck, or lose things. The Salish resisted the ideas of sin and hell, and at first seemed less interested in the Christian afterlife than in what Christian powers could do for them in this life.

Empire in the West

It seems that the idea of renewing the miracles of Paraguay amid those mountains was a Utopia. —Jan Roothaan, Superior General of the Society of Jesus, Rome, 1852

De Smet dreamed of establishing a peaceable "empire of Christian Indians" among the tribes of the eastern Plateau and Northern Rockies. Between 1841 and 1846, he founded missions and planted crosses of peace marking the corners of a far-flung wilderness kingdom.

It was the wrong century. Miners, settlers, military officers, and government treaty negotiators swiftly followed the missionaries. In less than twenty years, a tribal landscape punctuated only occasionally by trading posts, churches, and mission farms became the scene of warfare and dispossession.

De Smet's missionary career ended in 1848 when he was called back from the Rocky Mountains to become an administrator for the Missouri Jesuits. In later years, he used his fund-raising and recruitment talents to aid the Northwest missions, traveling to Europe seven times to beg men and money from noble and ecclesiastical patrons.

De Smet also continued to visit the Plains and Plateau tribes during the 1850s and 1860s, serving periodically as a government peace envoy. Convinced that peace treaties and permanent Indian reservations were the only alternative to extinction, De Smet urged the Sioux to place themselves under the government's protection and to sign the Fort Laramie treaties of 1851 and 1868.

The Cross of Peace on the Summit of the Rocky Mountains at the Source of the Columbia and Saskatchewan Rivers
Nicolas Point, S.J.
America, ca. 1841–47
graphite on paper
4 x 6⁷/₈ (10.2 x 17.5)
De Smetiana Collection, Jesuit Missouri Province Archives, St. Louis
IX-C9-36

De Smet was increasingly aware that the government did not keep its treaty promises. Having witnessed the destruction of the buffalo and the sudden collapse of the free Indian way of life, however, he could not imagine how the Plains tribes could survive the onslaught of white settlement without government help and protection.

Letters from his trips were published as books or pamphlets and were widely read on both sides of the Atlantic. Friend of fur traders, generals, bishops, presidents, Indian chiefs, and European nobility, De Smet won international fame during his lifetime.

Outsiders in America

De Smet spent the last thirty-five years of his life in St. Louis. Although he used his influence to counter the strong anti-Catholic undercurrent of white nineteenth-century America, he could not deter President Ulysses S. Grant from adopting an Indian peace policy after the Civil War that assigned Protestant missionaries across most of the West, even to tribes that requested or already had Catholic missionaries.

Although he worked for twenty years toward a just treaty settlement with the Sioux, at the end of his life, De Smet expressed doubts about the intentions of the government he had so willingly served. It may have seemed that both Indians and Catholics were outsiders in America. De Smet died in 1873, at the age of seventy-two.

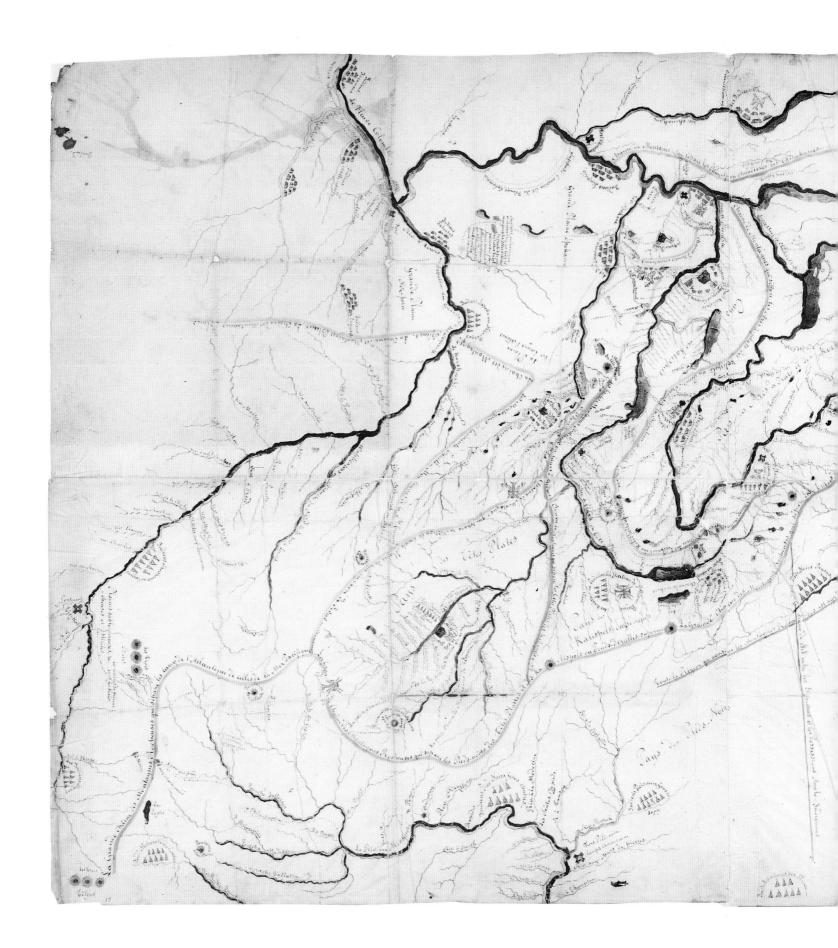

118

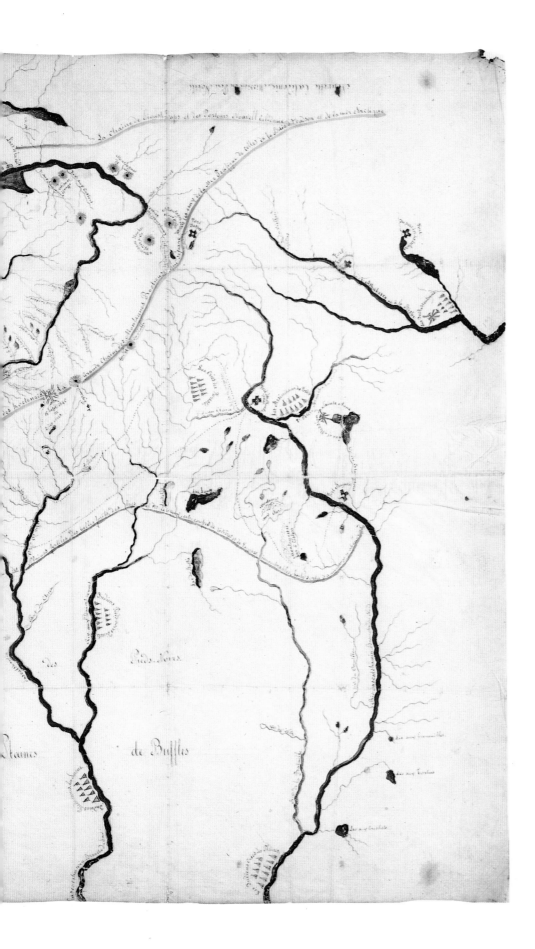

Map of Northern Rocky Mountains and Plateau
Pierre-Jean De Smet
America, ca. 1842–48
colored inks on paper
20½ x 34 (52.1 x 86.4)
De Smetiana Collection,
Jesuit Missouri Province
Archives, St. Louis
IX-C8-13

Despite inaccuracies in the general geographical orientation of this map, numerous Indian villages and campsites, missions, forts, trails, hot springs, mountain ranges, and watersheds, as well as tribal boundaries, are accurately plotted, testifying to De Smet's considerable knowledge of the geography and human cultures of the Northern Plains and Columbia Plateau.

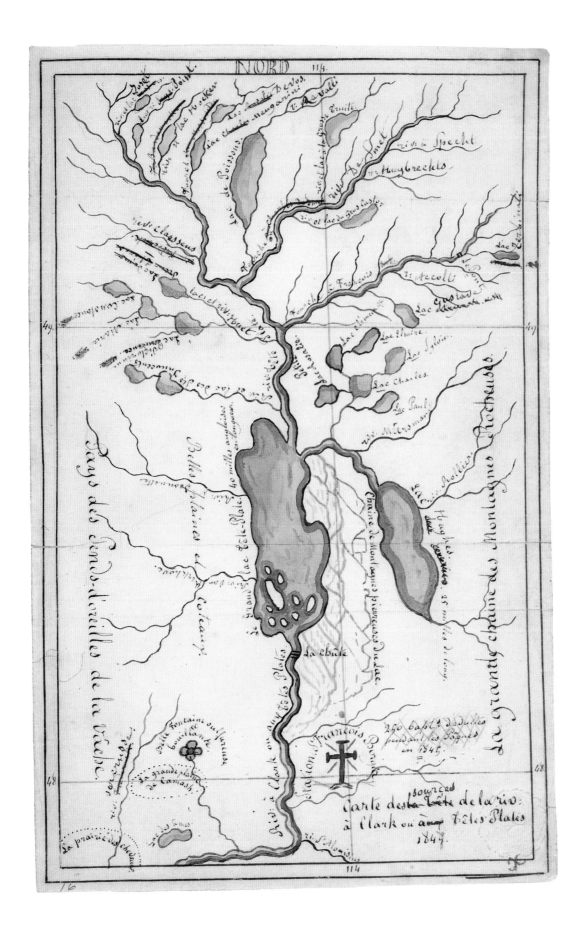

Source of the Flathead River

Pierre-Jean De Smet
America, 1847
colored inks on paper
5¼ x 8 (13.3 x 20.3)
De Smetiana Collection,
Jesuit Missouri Province
Archives, St. Louis
IX-C8-14A

In 1847 the Flathead
River–Flathead Lake re-
gion was occupied by the
Pend Oreille. After 1855,
the area would be set
aside as a reservation
for the Salish and Pend
Oreille. De Smet accu-
rately located four signifi-
cant gathering points:
the horse-grazing plains,
the camas prairie, the
hot springs, and the
Jesuit mission.

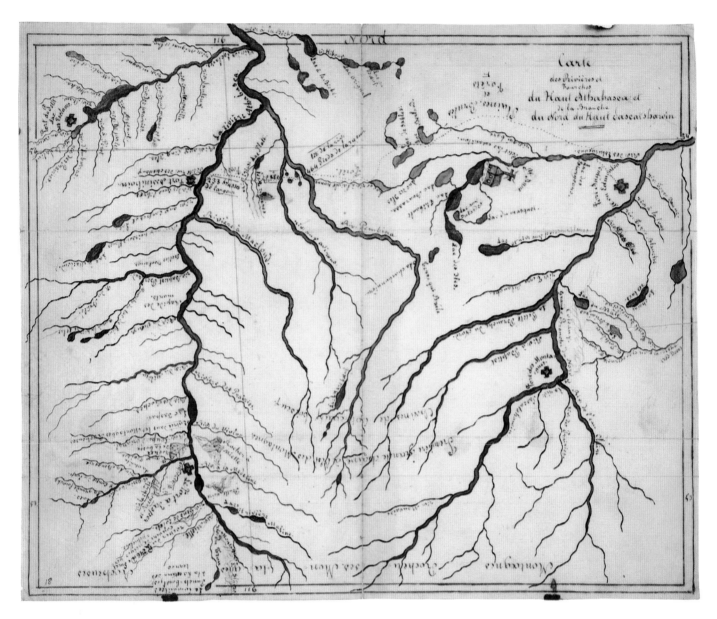

Map of the Upper Athabasca and Upper Saskatchewan Rivers
probably by Pierre-Jean De Smet
America, ca. 1846
colored inks on paper
8½ x 10¼ (21.6 x 26)
De Smetiana Collection, Jesuit Missouri Province Archives, St. Louis
IX-C8-15

In 1846 De Smet traveled across the Canadian Rockies in hopes of finding the Blackfeet and persuading them to accept Jesuit missionaries. He visited St. Anne's mission and the trading community at Fort Edmonton, but he did not find the Blackfeet. This map charts a portion of the journey.

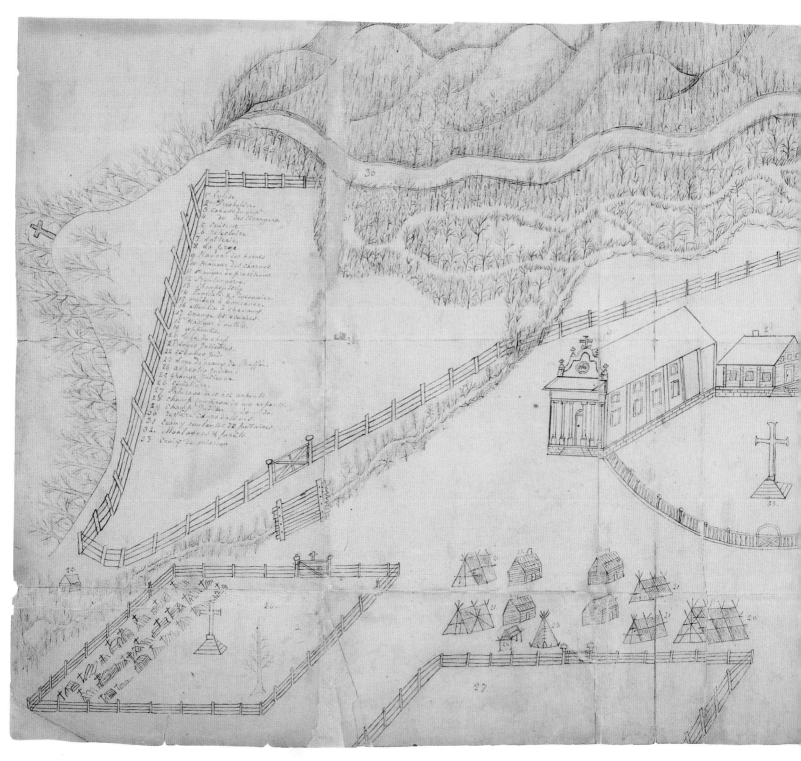

Sacred Heart Mission among the Coeur d'Alene
Pierre-Jean De Smet
America, ca. 1859–60
sepia ink on paper
11¼ x 21 (28.6 x 53.3)
De Smetiana Collection,
Jesuit Missouri Province
Archives, St. Louis
IX-C9-2

This bird's-eye view of the Sacred Heart mission to the Coeur d'Alene drawn by De Smet on his 1859 journey to the Northwest lacks perspective but provides considerable detail. An annotated key of thirty-three reference points locates mission buildings, Indian lodges, mission fields and pastures, and the Coeur d'Alene River.

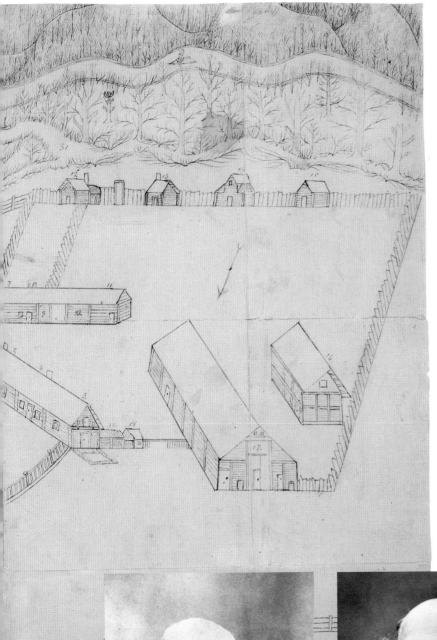

Joseph Joset, S.J., ca. 1880

Oregon Province Archives of the Society of Jesus, Crosby Library, Gonzaga University, Spokane, Washington

OPA 1353-7-8F

Joseph Joset, a Swiss Jesuit recruited by De Smet, arrived at the Sacred Heart mission to the Coeur d'Alene in November 1844. He would serve the Coeur d'Alene until his death in 1900, mastering their language and assisting the United States government in bringing peace to the Plateau during the Coeur d'Alene and Yakima wars of 1857–58.

Anthony Ravalli, S.J., ca. 1880

Oregon Province Archives of the Society of Jesus, Crosby Library, Gonzaga University, Spokane, Washington

OPA 1638-21F

Anthony Ravalli arrived in the Northwest in 1843. He assisted Gregory Mengarini at the Flathead mission and designed the new mission church among the Coeur d'Alene. He returned to St. Mary's when it reopened in 1866. A talented artist and sculptor, Ravalli also functioned as a physician and surgeon and a furniture maker.

Gregory Mengarini, S.J., ca. 1880

Oregon Province Archives of the Society of Jesus, Crosby Library, Gonzaga University, Spokane, Washington OPA VERT 115

Gregory Mengarini, born to a Roman patrician family in 1811, was, at twenty-nine, the youngest member of De Smet's original party. He served the Flathead mission from 1841 to 1850, when St. Mary's was closed. Mengarini was a gifted musician and linguist as well as a surgeon.

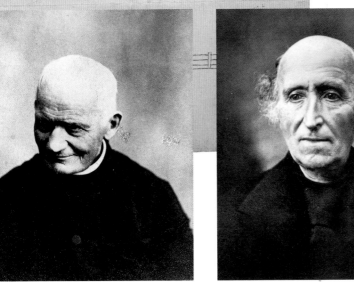

De Smet's Coat
Plains or Plateau,
ca. 1840–59
Indian tanned leather,
wool, silk, metal, thread,
pigment
41 x 40 (104.1 x 101.6)
Museum of the Western
Jesuit Missions, Florissant,
Missouri 990.8

The tribal origin of this
European-style coat re-
putedly made for De
Smet is a mystery. The
painted vine and cutouts
of leaves and berries,
backed by green and red
trade cloth, may have
been adapted from a
chalice design or the bor-
der of a stole worn by
De Smet during Mass.
The cutouts suggest east-
ern Plateau, Métis, or
Plains Cree manufacture.

Paper Crucifix
possibly made by
Pierre-Jean De Smet
America, ca. 1841–70
paper, glue, ink
7 x 3⅞ (17.8 x 9.8)
De Smetiana Collection,
Jesuit Missouri Province
Archives, St. Louis
IX-C-10

De Smet used this por-
table crucifix while on
missions among the Indi-
ans and presented it as
a token of esteem to one
of his altar boys in St.
Louis in 1870.

De Smet with Chiefs at Fort Vancouver, 1859
De Smetiana Collection, Jesuit Missouri Province Archives, St. Louis
IX-L2-A

At the urging of the Jesuit missionaries, most of the eastern Plateau tribes remained aloof from the Plateau war of 1858. Only the Coeur d'Alene engaged in actual combat. In 1859 De Smet brought friendly tribal leaders to Fort Vancouver to meet with General Harney. Left to right, front row: Victor, Kalispel; Alexander, Pend Oreille; Adolphe, Flathead; Andrew Seppline, Coeur d'Alene. Back row: Dennis, Colville; Bonaventure, Coeur d'Alene; De Smet; and Francis Xavier, Flathead.

Voyages aux montagnes rocheuses et une année de séjour chez les tribus indiennes de R. P. Pierre de Smet
Belgium, 1844
leather, paper, ink, silk
6⁷/8 x 4⁵/8 x 1 (17.5 x 11.8 x 2.5)
Jozef Dauwe, Lebbeke, Belgium

This first French edition of De Smet's collected letters from the Rocky Mountain missions, later published in English as *Letters and Sketches, with a Narrative of a Year's Residence among the Indians of the Rocky Mountains*, brought the exciting story of a European missionary's travels among the remote Rocky Mountain tribes to an eager European lay Catholic audience.

De Smet with Medal of the Order of Leopold

Petrus De Clerq
Belgium, ca. 1865–77
oil on textile
41¹⁵/₁₆ x 31⁷/₈ (106.5 x 81)
Kerkfabriek Onze-
Lieve-Vrouwekerk,
Dendermonde, Belgium

Although De Smet became a United States citizen in 1833, he maintained close ties with Flemish relatives and patrons. The government of Belgium recognized the contributions of its native son in 1865 by making De Smet a knight of the Order of Leopold, named for the first Belgian king.

Woman's Dress
Plains (Blackfeet) or
Plateau, collected by
Pierre-Jean De Smet,
1859
Indian tanned leather,
glass pony beads, shells,
wool, sinew, glass seed
beads, porcupine quills,
metal thimble
58³/₈ x 65¹/₄ (148.2 x
165.8)
Private collection,
Belgium

This dress was one of
several presents sent by
De Smet to Belgian rela-
tives and patrons follow-
ing the meeting in 1859
between General Harney
and Plateau chiefs at Fort
Vancouver. The cut of the
yoke, the pony-bead cir-
cles at the shoulders,
and the uneven hem line
all suggest Blackfeet
manufacture. De Smet
may have acquired the
dress on his return trip
to St. Louis at Fort
Benton, on the upper
Missouri River.

Unstuffed Pad Saddle
Plateau or Plains,
collected by Pierre-Jean
De Smet, 1859
Indian tanned leather,
glass seed beads, wool,
cotton, silk, faceted
glass beads, sinew
26¹/₂ x 24³/₄ (67.3 x 62.8)
Private collection,
Belgium

The bisymmetrical
beaded corner designs
on this unstuffed man's
saddle, with their in- and
out-curved spirals and
stylized flower and leaf
forms, are simplified re-
productions, produced at
a distance, of the more
elaborate multipart floral
designs and solidly
beaded corners made by
Plains Cree and Ojibwa
women.
    The cross-fertilization
of forms and motifs on
the Plateau and Northern
Plains makes secure
identification of such
pieces difficult.

Quilled Pouch
Plateau or Plains,
collected by Pierre-Jean
De Smet, 1859
Indian tanned leather,
porcupine quills, sinew
7³/₈ x 3¹/₂ (18.7 x 8.9)
Private collection,
Belgium

Shaped like a beaver tail,
this unusual hide pouch
is quilled in multicolored
checks, placed horizon-
tally on one side and in
chevrons on the other,
and edged with braided
quills. Although the raw
upper edge suggests
the pouch might have
been attached to some-
thing else, more likely its
maker designed it as a
tobacco pouch and sim-
ply did not finish it.

Brass Crucifix
Europe, mid-19th century
brass, wood
3³/₈ x 1⁵/₈ (8.6 x 4.1)
State Historical Society
of North Dakota (State Historical Board), Bismarck
5372

While at Sitting Bull's camp
in June 1868, De Smet presented this crucifix to American Horse, a principal war
leader of the Sioux. A similar cross was given to Two
Bears.

**Sitting Bull with
Crucifix, ca. 1885**
National Anthropological
Archives, Smithsonian
Institution, Washington,
D.C. 3193-A

De Smet gave Sitting
Bull this crucifix as a sign
of the fervent hope,
which both men shared,
that the power of the
Great Spirit would bring
peace and security to the
Sioux people.

**De Smet and Sioux
Indian Delegation at
Washington, D.C.,
ca. 1867**
Missouri Historical
Society, St. Louis
GARDNER 192

De Smet had a special
affection for the Sioux,
among whom he had
hoped to establish a per-
manent Jesuit mission.
He urged the government
to aid them in the transition from a hunting to a
sedentary way of life.

**De Smet's 1868 Peace
Mission to Sitting
Bull's Camp**
attributed to Matthew
Hastings
America, mid-19th century
watercolor on paper
8¾ x 11 (22.2 x 27.9)
De Smetiana Collection,
Jesuit Missouri Province
Archives, St. Louis IX-C7

In 1868 Eagle Woman,
the Hunkpapa Sioux wife
of interpreter Charles
Galpin, led De Smet to
Sitting Bull's camp. De
Smet's mission as a gov-
ernment envoy was to
persuade the Sioux to
sign the Fort Laramie
treaty. Seated under a
Marian banner, which he
gave to the Sioux as a
"holy emblem of peace,"
De Smet won the agree-
ment of Sitting Bull.
Camp leaders signed,
but peace did not last.

De Smet's Crucifix
Europe, mid-19th century
wood, ivory, metal
21¹/₄ x 7¹/₄ (54 x 18.4)
Museum of the Western
Jesuit Missions, Floris-
sant, Missouri 991.2

This finely carved crucifix
stood in De Smet's room
until his death in 1873.

Yankton Calumet
Plains (Yankton),
ca. 1858
wood, sinew, horsehair,
porcupine quills, thread,
catlinite
39³/₈ x 4³/₈ (100 x 11.1)
Private collection,
Belgium

In Plains Indian religion,
the calumet, or peace
pipe, is the visible sign
of communion with the
Great Holy, or Great
Spirit, and is the equiva-
lent of the Eucharist in
the Christian tradition.
This pipe belonged to

Padanin Apapi, Strikes
the Ree, a prominent
Yankton chief, who pre-
sented it to De Smet in
1857.

The Surrounded

Suffering for Indian people seems to have been a steady, healthy diet. Suffering became a way of life and suffering became the journey to survival. —Clifford SiJohn, Coeur d'Alene, 1992

Eneas and Man-am-ee Girl
Denver Public Library, Western History Department, Denver BS 115

While unwilling to surrender his traditional ways, this father understood the need of the young to adapt to white society. Wearing the Victorian dress of the late nineteenth century, his daughter stands on the threshold between two cultures.

St. Ignatius Mission
Peter Tofft
America, 1866
watercolor on paper
12½ x 20⅛ (31.7 x 51.1)
Montana Historical Society, Museum Purchase, Helena x62.05.01

The St. Ignatius mission to the Pend Oreille was originally located in northern Idaho. In 1854 it was moved to the Jocko Valley at the foot of Flathead Lake. Following the 1855 treaty, some of the Bitterroot Salish moved to the vicinity of St. Ignatius mission, then located within the new Flathead Reservation.

In the second half of the nineteenth century, the tribes of the Northern Rockies and eastern Plateau signed treaties under duress ceding their lands to the United States government. They became captives on reservations, subject to policies meant to destroy their culture and transform them into Americans. Mission schools forbade Indian children to speak their own language, and the federal government banned tribal religious ceremonies. The General Allotment Act opened the reservations to white settlement.

In a few terrible decades, the Salish and Coeur d'Alene lost their freedom and most of the land reserved to them by treaty. As game and roots became harder to find, many families turned to farming and ranching. They survived not only by adopting new economic strategies but also by clinging to the core of their identity and heritage, making these dark years a time of artistic creativity and cultural survival. Plateau decorative arts literally flowered during the late nineteenth century. The complex, abstract floral designs that evolved during these years asserted a continuing Indian identity, even while white Americans pressured the Salish and Coeur d'Alene to adopt their ways.

White settlers continued to look jealously at uncultivated Indian lands. In 1887 Congress passed the General Allotment Act. Disguised as a way to give Indian families title to their own 160-acre farms, the act opened up so-called surplus reservation lands to white settlers, who flocked to the Flathead reservation in 1910 and to the Coeur d'Alene reservation in 1917.

Throughout Indian country, the allotment policy devastated tribal economies and resulted in an estimated loss of 500 million acres by tribes whose "reserved" lands supposedly were protected by treaty.

**"Council in Bitterroot
Valley, July, 1855"**
Gustavus Sohon
America, 1855
graphite and watercolor
on paper
9³/₁₆ x 12⁵/₈ (23.3 x 32.1)
Washington State Historical
Society, Tacoma SOHON 34

Private Sohon graphically
recorded the 1854–55 treaty
councils in which Washington territorial governor
Isaac I. Stevens threatened,
promised, and humiliated
Northwest chiefs into ceding their lands to the government. The Hellgate
treaty with the Flathead,
Kootenai, and Pend Oreille
drew nearly 1,200 Indians.
Under a bower of saplings,
the three tribes exchanged
25,000 acres for a reservation in the Jocko Valley.

**Victor, Chief of the
Flathead, 1864**
Bitter Root Valley His-
torical Society, Ravalli
County Museums,
Hamilton, Montana
P85-20-P426

Victor wears the military
coat and yellow sash
that Governor Stevens
gave him in 1855. At the
Hellgate treaty council,
Stevens named Victor
head chief of the com-
bined Flathead, Kootenai,
and Pend Oreille tribes.
Victor refused to move
his people to the Flat-
head Reservation, hoping
that the government
would create a reserva-
tion for the Salish in the
Bitterroot Valley.

right to hunt and fish in any
Indian country where they are now
entitled to hunt and fish under
existing treaties. Nor shall
anything in this agreement
be so construed as to deprive any
of said Indians, so removing to
the Jocko Reservation, from
selling all their improvements
in the Bitter Root Valley.

James A. Garfield
    Special Com. for the Removal of the
        Flatheads from the Bitter Root Valley

Charlot First Chief of the Flatheads
    His   mark
Arly Second Chief of the Flatheads
    His + mark
Adolphe Third Chief of the Flatheads
    His + mark

Witness to Contract & Signatures
Wm H Clagett
D G Swaim J. a. u/a
W F Sanders
J. A. Viall
B. F. Potts Governor
        I certify that I interpreted fully
and carefully the foregoing contract to the
three Chiefs of the Flatheads named above—
Witness to Signature
        Baptiste Robwanen
                Interpreter
B. F. Potts, Governor   His + Mark

---

in such portion of the Jocko Reservation, not already occupied by other Indians, as said chiefs may select.

Second. That the superintendent of Indian affairs for Montana Territory shall cause to be delivered to said Indians 600 bushels of wheat, the same to be ground into flour without cost to said Indians, and delivered to them in good condition during the first year after their removal, together with such potatoes and other vegetables as can be spared from the agency farm.

Third. That said superintendent shall, as soon as practicable, cause suitable portions of land to be inclosed and broken up for said Indians, and shall furnish them with a/sufficient number of agricultural implements for the cultivation of their grounds.

Fourth. That in carrying out the foregoing agreement as much as possible shall be done at the agency by the employés of the Government; and none of such labor or materials, or provisions furnished from the agency, shall be charged as money.

Fifth. The whole of the $5,000 in money now in the hands of the said superintendent, appropriated for the removal of said Indians, shall be paid to them in such form as their chiefs shall determine, except such portion as is necessarily expended in carrying out the preceding provisions of this agreement.

Sixth. That there shall be paid to said tribe of Flathead Indians the further sum of $50,000, as provided in the second section of the act above recited, to be paid in ten annual installments, in such manner and material as the President may direct; and no part of the payments herein promised shall in any way affect or modify the full right of said Indians to the payments and annuities now and hereafter due them under existing treaties.

Seventh. It is understood and agreed that this contract shall in no way interfere with the rights of any member of the Flathead tribe to take land in the Bitter Root Valley under the third section of the act above cited.

Eighth. And the party of the second part hereby agree and promise that when the houses have been built as provided in the first clause of this agreement they will remove the Flathead tribe to said houses (except such as shall take land in the Bitter Root Valley), in accordance with the third section of the act above cited, and will thereafter occupy the Jocko Reservation as their permanent home. But nothing in this agreement shall deprive said Indians of their full right to hunt and fish in any Indian country where they are now entitled to hunt and fish under existing treaties. Nor shall anything in this agreement be so construed as to deprive any of said Indians, so removing to the Jocko Reservation, from selling all their improvements in the Bitter Root Valley.

JAMES A. GARFIELD,
Special Commissioner for the Removal of the Flatheads
from the Bitter Root Valley.
CHARLOT, his x mark,
First Chief of the Flatheads.
ARLEE, his x mark,
Second Chief of the Flatheads.
ADOLF, his x mark,
Third Chief of the Flatheads.

Witness to contract and signatures:
WM. H. CLAGETT.
D. G. SWAIM, Judge Advocate, United States Army.
W. F. SANDERS.
J. A. VIALL.
B. F. POTTS, Governor.

I certify that I interpreted fully and carefully the foregoing contract to the three chiefs of the Flatheads named above.

his
BAPTISTE + ROBWANEN,
mark.
Interpreter.

Witness to signature:
B. F. POTTS, Governor.

Charlot, although his name or mark is affixed to the published agreement, declares that he never signed it or authorized the signing, and the original agreement confirms his statements. He has refused to leave the Bitter Root Valley, some 360 of the tribe remaining with him. Under the third section of the act of 1872 patents for 160 acres of land each were issued to 41 members of the tribe, and Major Ronan, their

---

Evidence of a Forged Agreement of Removal

handwritten agreement between the Flathead tribe and James A. Garfield, August 27, 1872
Record Group 75, Records of the Bureau of Indian Affairs, National Archives, Washington, D.C.

printed agreement between the Flathead tribe and James A. Garfield, August 27, 1872
"Select Committee to Examine into the Conditions of the Sioux and Crow Indians," *Senate Report No. 283*, 48th Congress, 1st sess. (serial 2174), pp. xvii–xviii

Under pressure from white settlers, an 1872 act of Congress ordered the removal of the Bitterroot Salish to the Flathead Reservation. Two subchiefs signed the handwritten draft of the contract with U.S. commissioner James A. Garfield, but Chief Charlo refused, saying: "I will never sign your paper. . . . My heart belongs to this valley. I will never leave it." When Garfield published the document, it falsely indicated that Charlo had signed it.

1884 Salish Delegation to Washington

National Anthropological Archives, Smithsonian Institution, Washington, D.C. 43,583

In 1884 Charlo and other Salish leaders journeyed to Washington to meet with the president. Despite the Garfield agreement, Charlo still believed his people would be allowed to remain in the Bitterroot Valley. He won the battle—but eventually lost the war. Seven years later, under government escort, his people rode the seventy miles to the Flathead Reservation.

I do not believe your promise.
All I want is enough ground for
my grave. —Charlo, 1889

Charlo's Band Leaves
St. Mary's, 1891
Cheney Cowles Museum,
Spokane, Washington

The Bitterroot Salish ap-
pear in this photograph
with General Henry
Carrington, sent by the
federal government to
"escort" them to the res-
ervation in 1891. After an
all-night prayer vigil and
feast, the Salish gathered
before the mission church.

Then, singing the *Dies*
Irae—"The Day of Wrath,"
a funeral dirge—they rode
away from their home
and onto the reservation.

St. Ignatius Chapel,
1884
Haynes Foundation Collec-
tion, Montana Historical
Society, Helena H-1346

During the late nineteenth
century, Catholic missionaries vigorously sought
to stamp out traditional
Salish practices and be-
liefs, such as the sweat
lodge and medicine bun-
dles. Despite the authori-
tarian attitude of the

church, many Salish de-
pended upon their Catho-
lic faith to help sustain
them in these unhappy
years.

Flour Sack from St. Ignatius Mills
America, 19th century
cotton, ink
25¹/₈ x 13 (63.8 x 32.9)
Oregon Province of the
Society of Jesus, Portland
SJ 127

The Jesuits established
the industrial boarding
school for Salish boys at
St. Ignatius and expected
it to be self-supporting.
The flour mill and mission
farm also served as models of an American work
ethic for the Salish to
emulate.

Bell from St. Ignatius
America, 19th century
brass, Indian tanned
leather, glass beads
2⁷/₈ x 3¹/₄ (7.3 x 8.2)
Department of Anthropology, University of Montana, Missoula 6564

The sound of the bell
from the St. Ignatius
church was a call to "civilization" as well as to
worship. The church became an agent of forced
change, in step with the
late nineteenth-century
government policy that
the Salish abandon their
culture and become like
whites.

**Flathead Group at
Jocko Agency, 1894**
Mansfield Library, University of Montana, Missoula
78-33

The federal Indian agency
was essential to the government policy of assimilation. Staffed by whites,
who served as models
of Euroamerican values
and morals, the agency
exposed Indians to white
standards and exerted
pressure on them to conform. The loss of the buffalo and restrictions
against traveling and

hunting off the reservation forced the Salish and
other Plateau tribes to
adopt Western-style clothing and woven fabrics,
which were provided as
rations by the agency.
Plaid woolens were a particularly popular government issue.

St. Ignatius Mission School, late 19th century
Mansfield Library, University of Montana, Missoula 78-35

The residential school established by the Jesuits for Salish boys at St. Ignatius separated the students "from the blighting influence of their savage environment" and trained them "in the habits of civilized life." When they left the school after years of speaking English, some young men had forgotten their own language and could not speak with their own parents.

Flathead Indian Band, 1884
Haynes Foundation Collection, Montana Historical Society, Helena H-1350

When Jesuits introduced band instruments to the Salish in the 1840s, they eagerly learned the new music, believing it to have power similar to their own songs. In 1860, however, when band music and instruments were reintroduced at St. Ignatius, the martial music impressed upon the students the superior attitude of European civilization.

On entering with the others he has to keep silent until he can speak English. . . .
Such boys as are able should alternately learn reading & writing & some trade.

St. Ignatius Boy's Workshop, 1880s
Montana Historical Society, Helena 950-725

Salish boys display their shop projects in this photograph of the St. Ignatius industrial school. All boys at the school necessarily learned a useful trade. Many acquired skills, such as carpentry and blacksmithing, that contributed to the reservation economy.

Regulations for the College Boy
Colville Mission, ca. 1860–1900
ink on paper
Oregon Province Archives of the Society of Jesus, Crosby Library, Gonzaga University, Spokane, Washington OPA 551-F8

Archives
California Province

~ Colville Mission

Regulations
for the College boys.

1. No boy more than 13 years old is to be admitted; nor any one not enjoying good health

2. On his entrance the new comer is to be kept apart from the others until entirely cleansed from vermin.

3. On entering with the others he has to keep silent until he can speak English, as no other language is permitted

4. No one is to employ any one of the boys without a permission from the superior who will notify of this the teacher or prefect.

5. Any two or three boys will not be employed in any work without previously consulting the teacher or prefect as to the conveniency of their companionship.

6. Such boys as are able should alternately learn reading & writing & some trade.

7. No boy is to go ragged a single hour.

8. The prefect is to keep them clean especially from vermin. he has therefore

Tipis Covered with Woven Cloth, 1906
Montana Historical Society, Helena 954-583

As buffalo hides became increasingly difficult to obtain, women turned to woven textiles such as canvas and mattress ticking for lodge covers. These Salish lodges are set against the background of the Mission Mountains.

Mose Vanderburg and Wife, ca. 1900
Denver Public Library, Western History Department, Denver BS 55

Mose Vanderburg plays a hand drum in front of the family's canvas-covered lodge while waiting for a meal. Although the food is made in "modern" equipment, the scene is a traditional one.

Lucy Pierre and Daughter on Horseback, 1906
Montana Historical Society, Helena 954-554

Despite the government's ban of Indian ceremonies, Indian people found ways to perpetuate tradition. On the Flathead Reservation, an annual Fourth of July powwow featured parades, dancing in traditional beaded regalia, singing, and gambling as additions to the agricultural fair encouraged by the agent. The women shown here are dressed for a parade or powwow.

Saddle Blanket
Plateau (Salish), ca. 1900
wool, glass seed beads,
metal, oil cloth, thread
48¾ x 32 (123.8 x 81.3)
Buffalo Bill Historical
Center, Cody, Wyoming,
Simplot collection, gift of
J. R. Simplot L.1.85.159 A

Horse Collar
Plateau (Salish), ca. 1900
wool, oil cloth, glass
seed beads, bells, Indian
tanned leather, thread
30¾ x 19½ (78.1 x 49.5)
Buffalo Bill Historical
Center, Cody, Wyoming,
Simplot collection, gift of
J. R. Simplot L.1.85.159 B

Horse Martingale
Plateau (Salish), ca. 1900
wool, oil cloth, glass seed
beads, bells, Indian
tanned leather, thread
51¼ x 6⅝ (130.2 x 16.8)
Buffalo Bill Historical
Center, Cody, Wyoming,
Simplot collection, gift of
J. R. Simplot L.1.85.159 C

Lavish and beautifully
beaded horse gear from
the turn of the century
affirms the continuing
importance of the horse
in Salish culture. This
stunning matched set of
saddle blanket, horse
collar, and martingale
was probably made by a
single artist. The sophisticated abstract floral de-
sign, depicting the life
cycle of a flowering plant
from seed to blossom, is
a fine example of classic
Salish beadwork. Salish
artists still show a prefer-
ence for black and navy
textiles against which to
show off colorful seed
bead patterns.

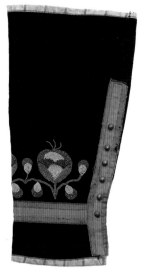

Woman's Beaded Leggings

Ellen Big Sam, maker
Plateau (Salish), ca. 1900
wool, cotton, silk, brass
tacks, metal snaps, shoe
buttons, glass seed
beads, thread
13 x 6¾ (33 x 17.2)
Four Winds Indian Trading
Post, Preston Miller col-
lection, St. Ignatius, Montana

Plateau women enthu-
siastically adopted
American technology,
such as the sewing ma-
chine, when it served
them. Ellen Big Sam used
a machine to sew the
bright ribbons on these
traditionally styled
women's leggings.

Beaded Man's Vest

Ellen Big Sam, maker
Plateau (Salish), ca. 1900
canvas, woven textile,
Indian tanned leather,
glass seed and tubular
beads, thread, metal
buckle
22¼ x 18¼ (56.5 x 46.3)
Four Winds Indian Trading
Post, Preston Miller Col-
lection, St. Ignatius, Montana

In the second half of the
nineteenth century, Indian
men began wearing non-
Indian clothing such as
vests, hats, pants, and
belts. Showing their flair
for combination and elab-
oration, Plateau women
took woven cloth and
embroidered it with both
realistic and abstract
floral designs.

Beaded Gauntlets

Ellen Big Sam, maker
Plateau (Salish), ca. 1900
leather, glass seed beads,
cotton, thread
12 x 6½ (30.5 x 16.5)
Four Winds Indian Trading
Post, Preston Miller
Collection, St. Ignatius,
Montana

On the Flathead and
Coeur d'Alene reserva-
tions, many men turned
to ranching and horse
breeding after 1880. Men
more likely wore fancy
gauntlets like these dur-
ing parades than at the
corral.

**Ellen Big Sam,
Salish Artist, early
20th century**
Mansfield Library, University of Montana, Missoula
76-41

Women's skills and artistic vision kept beadwork and Indian identity alive through the hardest decades. Ellen (Pierre) Big Sam, shown on the left with her sister, Mary Ann (Pierre) Combs, was a prolific and expert beader known for her abstract floral designs.

Two-sided Flat Bag
Plateau (Coeur d'Alene),
early 20th century
Indian tanned leather,
glass seed beads, brass
and wood crucifix, wool
yarn, woven textile,
cotton string, cornhusk,
hemp, thread
10⁹/₁₆ x 8³/₈ (26.8 x 21.4)
Cheney Cowles Museum,
Spokane, Washington
CASEY 81 1/10

Popular in the late nine-
teenth century, flat
beaded bags made from
imported textiles may
have been adapted from
flat, twined root bags
made from hemp or corn-
husk. This bag blends
two disciplines of the
eastern Plateau. The side
shown here is decorated
with stylized floral beadwork; the other is a cornhusk panel, which may
have been salvaged from
a damaged root bag.

Flat Beaded Bag
Plateau (Coeur d'Alene),
early 20th century
Indian tanned leather,
glass seed beads, metal
beads, cotton, thread
10 x 8¹/₈ (25.5 x 20.6)
Cheney Cowles Museum,
Spokane, Washington
ND 1361

Beginning in the late nineteenth century, Plateau
women made flat beaded
bags of various shapes
both for their personal
use and to sell. This bag
is a classic example of
Plateau pictorial beadwork,
which portrayed animals,
landscapes, people, or
patriotic symbols. The artist who made this bag
carefully crafted the bird's
image from small, faceted,
glass seed beads.

Cradleboard with Horses on Apron

Plateau, late 19th century
Indian tanned leather,
glass seed and tubular
beads, woven and knit
textile, wood, bells,
leather, thread, sinew
40 x 14¾ x 7⅜ (101.5 x
37.5 x 18.7)
McCord Museum of Canadian History, Montreal
ME 987.238A-C

Plateau women fashioned cradleboards from
rounded, cone-shaped
wood panels and covered
them with Indian tanned
leather. Unlike the cradleboards of other Plateau
tribes, Salish cradleboards have a uniformly
broad, almost rectangular
upper panel. In this example, the stylized leaf
and bud design on the
upper panel and the
pinto ponies on the
leather apron reflect classic Salish floral and pictorial motifs.

Woman Digging Roots, 20th century
Mansfield Library, University of Montana, Missoula 82-21

Despite increasing reliance on cultivated and store-bought foods and medicines, the Salish and Coeur d'Alene continue to supplement their diet and alleviate sickness with wild roots and plants. Women assume the task of digging roots, such as camas and bitterroot, which are still served at family and community feasts.

Flathead Sweathouse, early 20th century
Denver Public Library, Western History Department, Denver F40153

Survival of the sweathouse, a sacred place of prayer and purification, meant the survival of tribal spiritual traditions. Made of a bent willow frame and covered with skins, the sweathouse is still used by modern Plateau people.

Flathead Farm, ca. 1900
Hayes Foundation Collection, Montana Historical Society, Helena H-1339

By 1894 the Salish and Coeur d'Alene had made the transition to farming and ranching. Although few families had large operations, the prosperity of these Indian ranchers and farmers equaled that of their white counterparts in Montana and Idaho. The General Allotment Act was to change all that by breaking up extended family residential units and reducing Indian holdings to a mere 160 acres of often marginal land.

**Indians in Auto-
mobile, ca. 1920s**
Cheney Cowles Museum,
Spokane, Washington

Even after cars arrived on
the reservation, many
Indians continued to use
horses, but the automo-
bile created the same
excitement and extended
mobility among Indians
as it did among whites.

**Coeur d'Alene
Baseball Team, 1899**
Coeur d'Alene Tribe, His-
torical Testimony Pro-
gram, De Smet, Idaho

Traditional Indian games
helped Indian children
develop essential skills
for a hunting and gather-
ing economy. As times
changed and the neces-
sity for learning these
skills decreased, the
popularity of Euro-
american games such as
baseball grew. These
young men wear the uni-
form of the De Smet,
Idaho, team.

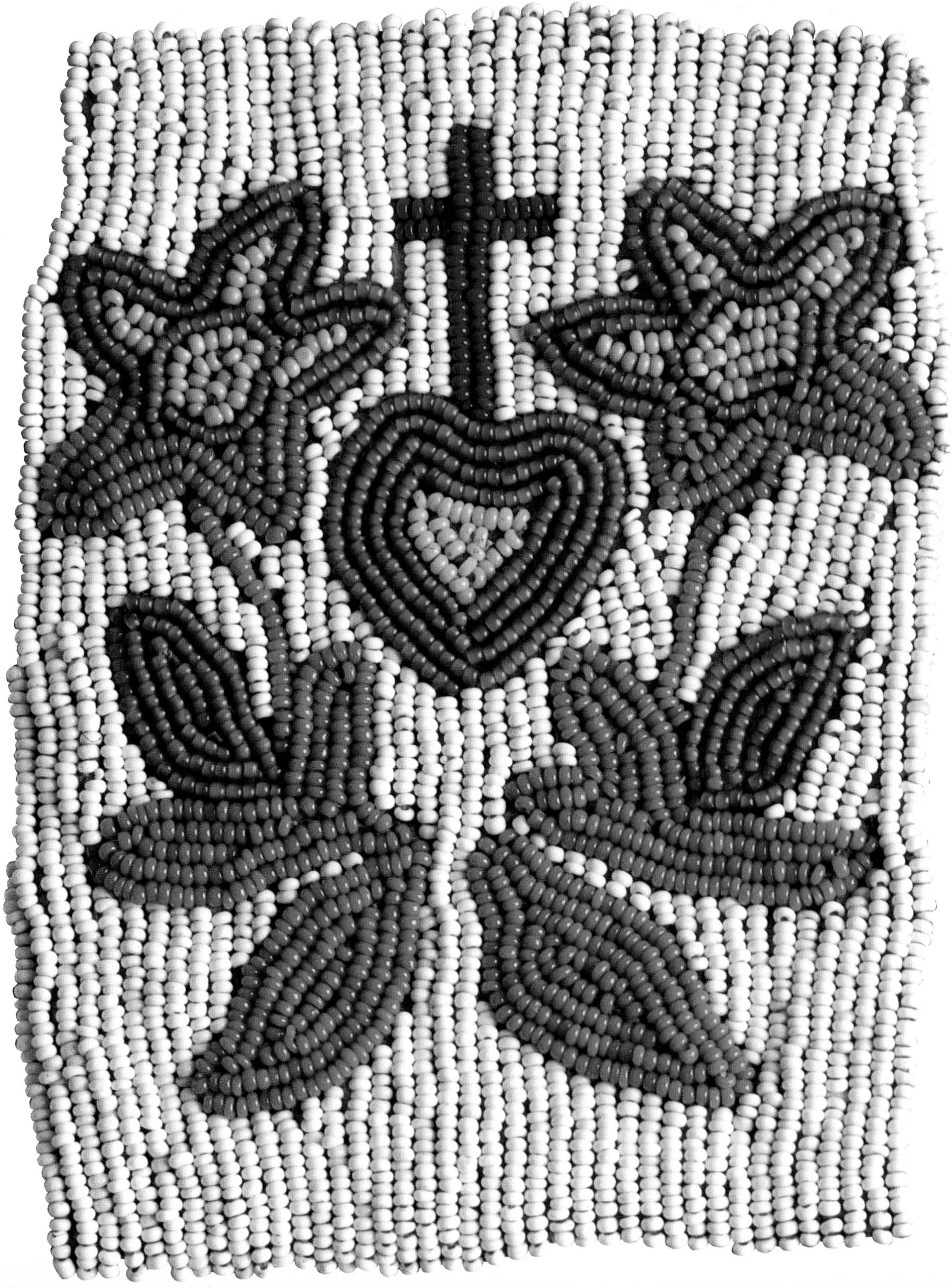

Flat Beaded Bag
Plateau (Coeur d'Alene),
ca. 1900
Indian tanned leather,
glass seed beads, cotton
thread
10 x 3 (25.4 x 7.6)
Cheney Cowles Museum,
Spokane, Washington
38x

A beadwork design that
grafts the Sacred Heart of
Jesus onto the stem of a
traditional floral motif
lovingly illustrates the
entwining of Indian and
Christian beliefs by Pla-
teau people. This small
bag may have been used
to carry the communion
wafer to the sick.

Shrine of St. Ignatius on the Flathead Reservation, 1907
Benjamin Stone, Denver Public Library, Western History Department
F42232

"The people strongly believed in the power of prayer so they continued going to the mission, continued learning about God. And they learned about this new man named Jesus, and they identified with him because he done many of the things our people done when they pray— he fasted and he suffered and he helped cure people. So our people strongly believed in him."—Clarence Woodcock, Director, Salish Culture Committee, 1992

De Smet Mission and Village in Winter, early 20th century
Coeur d'Alene Tribe, Historical Testimony Program, De Smet, Idaho

When the beautiful church at Cataldo fell outside the reservation boundaries, the Jesuits relocated the Sacred Heart mission to the Coeur d'Alene on a hillside they called De Smet. During Lent, Christmas, and on holy days, the Coeur d'Alene would travel from all parts of the reservation in wagons or by sleigh and camp in small cabins at the bottom of the hill. The cabins are gone now, but the Indians still call this place "camp."

MES NEW SETTLERS
NTANA

A HOME FOR YOU AND A FORTUNE, TOO ✔ ✔ ✔

The Lands of the Wonderful and Rich

Flathead Indian Reservation

In Western Montana

Are to be disposed of by the Government, to those persons who have not yet exercised their homestead rights.

The owner of one of these rich tracts of land will be the possessor of a home in one of the most desirable sections of the whole United States, in which to live, and its soil will yield an income each year which will make the owner independent.

Can you afford to let this opportunity go by without at least finding out something about it?

Think of it! There are 1,433,600 acres on the Flathead.

Do you want 160 acres of these lands?

We have just completed extensive arrangements for a new department, the benefits of which will go to all of our members and through the channels of it we shall place our members in closer touch with the opportunity of owning one of these homesteads.

A new plan for those persons who are not yet members has just been inaugurated and will be ready for presentation about January 10 next. Under this plan it will make it easy for YOU to become a member—so easy that unless you are satisfied with the rut you are now in or do not care to avail yourself of this remarkable offer of the Government, that you will do yourself an injustice if you don't write for our new booklet.

We have ordered but a limited supply of these booklets. They will be off the press about January 10. If you want one, you must write AT ONCE—TODAY!

As we said before, the supply is limited and your name will take the order in which it is received. Therefore, if you are in dead, hard earnest and want to own 160 acres of the richest land in the West; if you want to be put in touch with this real live opportunity, send us your name and address TODAY, being sure to ask for Booklet "P."

FLATHEAD RESERVATION INFORMATION AGENCY

DRAWER "F." . . . MISSOULA, MONT.

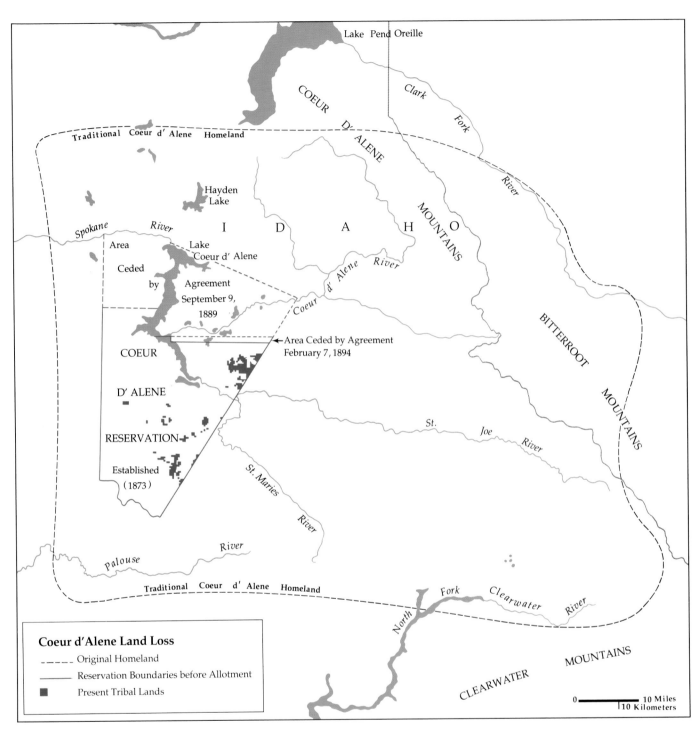

Lake Pend Oreille

Clark

Fork

COEUR D' ALENE

River

Traditional Coeur d' Alene Homeland

MOUNTAINS

Hayden Lake

Spokane   River

I D A H O

Coeur   d' Alene   River

Area

Lake Coeur d' Alene

Ceded

by   Agreement
           September 9,
           1889

BITTERROOT

Coeur d' Alene River

←Area Ceded by Agreement
   February 7, 1894

COEUR

MOUNTAINS

D' ALENE

RESERVATION←

St.   *Joe   River*

Established
(1873)

St. Maries

River

Palouse   River

Traditional   Coeur d' Alene   Homeland

North   Fork   Clearwater   River

CLEARWATER   MOUNTAINS

Coeur d'Alene Land Loss

- – – – Original Homeland
- ———— Reservation Boundaries before Allotment
- ■ Present Tribal Lands

0 ▬▬▬ 10 Miles
  ▬▬▬ 10 Kilometers

Land Loss through Treaty Cession and Allotment

These maps show the reduction over time of the ancestral lands of the Coeur d'Alene and the Flathead tribes. Immigration of whites into the area, forced treaty cessions, confinement onto small tracts, and eventual pressure by land-hungry whites to reduce these territories further through allotment—all contributed to a shrinking land base and a loss of power.

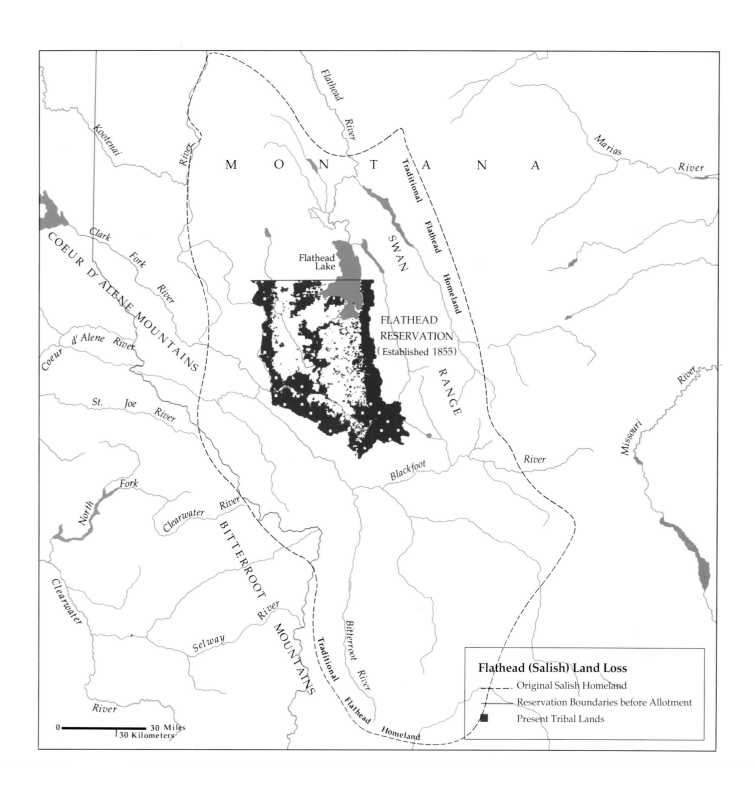

MONTANA

Kootenai
River

Clark Fork River

COEUR D' ALENE MOUNTAINS

Coeur d' Alene River

St. Joe River

North Fork

Clearwater River

BITTERROOT MOUNTAINS

Clearwater
River

Selway

River

Flathead River

Flathead Lake

Traditional Flathead Homeland

SWAN RANGE

Marias River

FLATHEAD
RESERVATION
(Established 1855)

Blackfoot River

Bitterroot River

Traditional Flathead Homeland

Missouri River

Traditional Flathead Homeland

0   30 Miles
       30 Kilometers

Flathead (Salish) Land Loss

– – – Original Salish Homeland

——— Reservation Boundaries before Allotment

■ Present Tribal Lands

Closing the Circle: The People Today

Long ago the promise of the river was that it would be life-giving for all. It represents for us a spiritual model, a model of a way of life. This is a law that has been here for a long time, for many thousands of years, and it is still here, just as the people are still here, and just as the river is still here. So I think the main message of . . . this display of sacred encounters is to communicate to people, wherever you are, that this way of life is still open to you, that a body of knowledge still exists. We are still here. —Peter Campbell, Lakes–Coeur d'Alene

Recent decades have witnessed the growth of a native Christianity and the revival of traditional Indian beliefs and practices throughout the Western Hemisphere. These developments, along with the apologies of Christian churches and the United States government, do not erase the pain and bitterness of the past five hundred years, but they are a beginning.

Clarence Woodcock, director of the Salish Culture Committee, wrote in 1992: "In the 1960s, the church began to recognize and know that our peoples' ceremonials, songs, and dances were good. The Vatican Council encouraged people to pray, to sing, and to dance in their own native ways. One of the greatest statements I heard was that Jesus takes on the countenance of whatever culture he is in. So this began a new awakening. And the people started going back to the circle."

A PUBLIC DECLARATION

TO THE TRIBAL COUNCILS AND TRADITIONAL SPIRITUAL LEADERS OF THE INDIAN AND ESKIMO PEOPLES OF THE PACIFIC NORTHWEST
In care of Jewell Praying Wolf James, Lummi

Seattle, Washington
November 21, 1987

Dear Brothers and Sisters,

This is a formal apology on behalf of our churches for their long-standing participation in the destruction of traditional Native American spiritual practices. We call upon our people for recognition of and respect for your traditional ways of life and for protection of your sacred places and ceremonial objects. We have frequently been unconscious and insensitive and have not come to your aid when you have been victimized by unjust Federal policies and practices. In many other circumstances we reflected the rampant racism and prejudice of the dominant culture with which we too willingly identified. During the 200th Anniversary year of the United States Constitution we, as leaders of our churches in the Pacific Northwest, extend our apology. We ask for your forgiveness and blessing.

As the Creator continues to renew the earth, the plants, the animals and all living things, we call upon the people of our denominations and fellowships to a commitment of mutual support in your efforts to reclaim and protect the legacy of your own traditional spiritual teachings. To that end we pledge our support and assistance in upholding the American Religious Freedom Act (P.L. 95-134, 1978) and within that legal precedent affirm the following:

1) The rights of the Native Peoples to practice and participate in traditional ceremonies and rituals with the same protection offered all religions under the Constitution.

2) Access to and protection of sacred sites and public lands for ceremonial purposes.

3) The use of religious symbols (feathers, tobacco, sweet grass, bones, etc.) for use in traditional ceremonies and rituals.

The spiritual power of the land and the ancient wisdom of your indigenous religions can be, we believe, great gifts to the Christian churches. We offer our commitment to support you in the righting of previous wrongs: To protect your peoples' efforts to enhance Native spiritual teachings; to encourage the members of our churches to stand in solidarity with you on these important religious issues; to provide advocacy and mediation, when appropriate, for ongoing negotiations with State agencies and Federal officials regarding these matters.

May the promises of this day go on public record with all the congregations of our communions and be communicated to the Native American Peoples of the Pacific Northwest. May the God of Abraham and Sarah, and the Spirit who lives in both the cedar and Salmon People be honored and celebrated.

Sincerely,

The Rev. Thomas L. Blevins, Bishop
Pacific Northwest Synod –
    Lutheran Church in America

The Rev. Dr. Robert Bradford,
    Executive Minister
American Baptist Churches of the Northwest

The Rev. Robert Brock
N.W. Regional Christian Church

The Right Rev. Robert H. Cochrane,
    Bishop, Episcopal Diocese of Olympia

The Rev. W. James Halfaker
Conference Minister
Washington North Idaho Conference
    United Church of Christ

The Most Rev. Raymond G. Hunthausen
    Archbishop of Seattle
Roman Catholic Archdiocese of Seattle

The Rev. Elizabeth Knott, Synod Executive
Presbyterian Church
    Synod Alaska-Northwest

The Rev. Lowell Knutson, Bishop
North Pacific District
    American Lutheran Church

The Most Rev. Thomas Murphy
    Coadjutor Archbishop
Roman Catholic Archdiocese of Seattle

The Rev. Melvin G. Talbert, Bishop
United Methodist Church –
    Pacific Northwest Conference

Public Declaration of Apology to Northwest Native People
signed by ten bishops and denominational leaders on November 21, 1987
Native American Task Force, The Church Council of Greater Seattle

**American Indian
Religious Freedom
Act**
Public Law 95-341, Joint
Resolution of the 95th
Congress, August 11, 1978

PUBLIC LAW 95–341—AUG. 11, 1978

92 STAT. 469

Public Law 95–341
95th Congress

Joint Resolution

American Indian Religious Freedom.

Aug. 11, 1978
[S.J. Res. 102]

Whereas the freedom of religion for all people is an inherent right, fundamental to the democratic structure of the United States and is guaranteed by the First Amendment of the United States Constitution;

Whereas the United States has traditionally rejected the concept of a government denying individuals the right to practice their religion and, as a result, has benefited from a rich variety of religious heritages in this country;

Whereas the religious practices of the American Indian (as well as Native Alaskan and Hawaiian) are an integral part of their culture, tradition and heritage, such practices forming the basis of Indian identity and value systems;

Whereas the traditional American Indian religions, as an integral part of Indian life, are indispensable and irreplaceable;

Whereas the lack of a clear, comprehensive, and consistent Federal policy has often resulted in the abridgment of religious freedom for traditional American Indians;

Whereas such religious infringements result from the lack of knowledge or the insensitive and inflexible enforcement of Federal policies and regulations premised on a variety of laws;

Whereas such laws were designed for such worthwhile purposes as conservation and preservation of natural species and resources but were never intended to relate to Indian religious practices and, therefore, were passed without consideration of their effect on traditional American Indian religions;

Whereas such laws and policies often deny American Indians access to sacred sites required in their religions, including cemeteries;

Whereas such laws at times prohibit the use and possession of sacred objects necessary to the exercise of religious rites and ceremonies;

Whereas traditional American Indian ceremonies have been intruded upon, interfered with, and in a few instances banned: Now, therefore, be it

Resolved by the Senate and House of Representatives of the United States of America in Congress assembled, That henceforth it shall be the policy of the United States to protect and preserve for American Indians their inherent right of freedom to believe, express, and exercise the traditional religions of the American Indian, Eskimo, Aleut, and Native Hawaiians, including but not limited to access to sites, use and possession of sacred objects, and the freedom to worship through ceremonials and traditional rites.

American
Indian Religious
Freedom.
42 USC 1996.

**Lawrence Aripa,
Coeur d'Alene**

"You just get with it . . . the beat of the drum. You sometimes get the feeling that you're back like in the old days, you know. For a brief moment, you're high up there. You're really feeling good—'I'm an Indian! I'm an Indian!'"

Agnes Kenmille, Salish

"My mother was three years old when they had to leave the Bitterroot. They were bitter, the people. It's sad for them. They still talk about it. They think about what happened because that was the Indians' church. That's where they go to Mass on Sunday, whenever they have wakes or something like that. That's where the cemetery is, right there for the Indians."

Lucy Finley, Coeur d'Alene
"On my stone I'd like to have a rainbow with a star and the moon. And under the rainbow, it says, 'I danced for my people. And now I am dancing with the Spirit.' So there'd be tipis here and a sweat lodge here. That's my picture on my stone. I don't know if I'll get it, but that's my dream."

**Clarence Woodcock,
Pend Oreille**

"I was always around a lot of old people, speaking our language, and just kind of living a real traditional life. I remember every night, especially during Lent, we'd have to pray the whole rosary sometimes, of course in our Salish language. Church every Sunday and sweats all the time, and just having . . . a lot of people there all the time is what made it so secure."

Louis Adams, Salish

"Like I was telling you about the Bible. I looked through that and didn't see anything bad in it. I went to medicine dances all my life and I never seen anything bad in it, because it all has to do with life, the future, the future of your people. It has to do with preservation, with respect."

Frances Vanderburg, Salish

"When the Black Robes got here is when my ancestors were run out of their homeland. But they still hung on to the Catholic ways. They used the sweat house, they used their medicine dances, but kind of on the sideline and then they'd go to church. My amazement is that after all that happened, they still stayed Catholic. It made some people strong."

Clifford SiJohn, Coeur d'Alene
"My grandmother used to tell us, 'You speak from the heart, your hands will be clean, all your life.' So when we sing, it comes out clean. It's beautiful. It's pure. And it'll last forever."

Louise Combs, Salish

"What's an Indian? I really don't know what to say about that because being an Indian, seems like nobody wants to listen to us. But now, our children are going to colleges and universities. They're the ones that are seeing how we were treated, and they're working against that now."

**John Peter Paul,
Pend Oreille**

"I believe in both the ways. If I ask my Spirit for something I usually get it. You talk to God, you ask him something, you'll get it too."

**Justine Vincent,
Coeur d'Alene**

Justine Vincent, the "sweetheart of the Coeur d'Alene tribe" who loved to dance, passed away on October 6, 1992. She was eighty-seven. This photograph was taken at the war dance following Mass at Cataldo mission on the Feast of the Assumption, August 15, 1991.

Acknowledgments

This book, like the exhibition it documents, is about people instead of things. Many of the objects in the exhibition are breathtaking. Some are powerful embodiments of the religious. Worked by human hands in the medium of culture, all reflect the human spirit. But, while the objects "speak," they do not speak to everyone or in the same cultural language. What the objects "mean" is really an extension of what the people who made them "mean," or meant. When people from radically different cultures get together, the chances of misunderstanding or missing the meaning altogether are very good.

The Pierced Heart Singers
Four generations of SiJohn family members from the Coeur d'Alene tribe, in a recording session for an audio track for *Sacred Encounters.*

Sacred Encounters examines the historic encounter and dialogue between peoples whose meanings rose out of two radically different world views. That both worlds were sacred to their inhabitants did not make the dialogue any clearer or the parties any more equal in one another's eyes. The potential for misunderstanding, condescension, manipulation, or oppression was always present, just as it is still present wherever groups or individuals face one another across a cultural, religious, gender, racial, or ethnic divide. We can invade but we cannot inhabit one another's skins.

In the making of *Sacred Encounters,* hundreds of talented individuals—Native American scholars, elders, and tradition bearers; Jesuits, diocesan priests, and Catholic Indian leaders; humanities scholars, museum directors, curators, registrars, and conservators; artists, musicians, craftsmen, filmmakers, photographers, editors, and designers; university researchers, administrators, accountants, and support staff all worked together, seeking a common expression of a complex human story. We were not always successful, and, as director, I assume responsibility for the times when we were not. But, collectively, we produced something extraordinarily honest and humane. Both the exhibition and the book are nourishment for the soul, as well as for the eyes and mind.

Sacred Encounters began in a chance encounter with William B. Faherty, S.J., archivist of the Jesuit Missouri Province Archives; St. Louis. His generous spirit and confidence literally buoyed the exhibition into existence. Father Faherty, his associate archivist Nancy Merz, and many other Jesuits believed in the worth of the exhibition and were willing to risk, in the hands of a lay scholar specializing in Native American history, a close examination both of the nineteenth-century Jesuit mission to the tribes of the northern Rockies and of Father De Smet, a heroic figure in Catholic-American history. I want to thank Cornelius Buckley, S.J., Thomas Connolly, S.J., Francis Guentner, S.J., John Killoren, S.J., Thomas Lucas, S.J., Maurice McNamee, S.J., Gerald McKevitt, S.J., John Padberg, S.J., and Joseph Retzel, S.J., for sharing their knowledge and wisdom with me. Jesuit archivists Joseph Cossette and Robert Toupin, St-Jérôme, Québec; Neill R. Meany, Spokane, Washington; and J. E. Windey, Brussels, assisted in the search for documents and artifacts. Thomas M. Rochford, S.J., gave his friendship, sage counsel, and a set of landscape photographs that see God in all things.

The search for De Smet–related materials led to the Belgian Embassy in Washington, D.C. I am grateful to Andrea Murphy for her many helpful suggestions, and to former Ambassador Herman Dehennin and current Ambassador Juan Cassiers for their interested support of the exhibition. I was warmly received on three occasions by De Smet family members in Belgium, as well as by officials, clerics, and private citizens in Dendermonde, De Smet's birthplace. I want to thank Aimé Stroobants, archivist of the Stedelijke Musea, Dendermonde, for locating and coordinating numerous Belgian loans. I am also grateful to Louis De Stryker, for professional advice, and to Dom Bernard Daeleman, o.s.b., the city of Dendermonde, A. Derveaux of the Kerkfabriek-Onze-Lieve Vroewekerk, Sir Josse de Smet d'Olbecke, and, especially, Jozef Dauwe and his family for their kind hospitality.

Similarly, the exhibition and this book could not have come about without the sanction of the tribal councils of the Confederated Salish and Kootenai Tribes and the Coeur d'Alene Tribe, and the support and guidance of the Salish Culture Committee, under the direction of Clarence Woodcock. During the past five years, Clarence Woodcock and many other Salish, Coeur d'Alene, Pend Oreille, and Spokane elders, tradition bearers, and scholars have been my teachers and friends. They risked what some feared might be a violation of the sacred ways of the Salish. Several said that they did so believing that the exhibition would help to heal their people by exposing the pain of the past and by restoring pride in Indian traditions. For sharing their advice and traditions with me and Larry Johnson, the exhibition's audiovisual producer, I especially want to thank Louis Adams, Lawrence Aripa, Joanne Bigcrane, Peter Campbell, Victor Charlo, Debra Earling, Julie Cajune Holt, Clifford SiJohn, Frances Vanderburg, and Betty White. I am also grateful to Myrna Adams, Felix Aripa, Vivian and Hank Baylor, Art Bigcrane, Louise Combs, Rose Goddard, Germaine DuMontier, Greg DuMontier, Lucy Finley, Agnes Kenmille, Dolly Linseberger, Lawrence Nicodemus, Millie Nicodemus, John Peter Paul, Dixie Sehler, Bingo SiJohn, and Harriet Whitworth. Thanks also to Johnny Arlee for collaboration in the selection of Salish music, and to Robert Bigart,

Corwin Clairmont, Gerald Slater, Joyce Silverthorne, Frank Tyro, and Roy Bigcrane of Salish Kootenai College for advice as well as library, administrative, and media support.

Sacred Encounters was organized from a university rather than a museum base, and a number of individuals and departments at Washington State University made this unusual effort possible. I am grateful to my colleagues Allan Smith, Plateau scholar and former Chair of the Department of Anthropology; Loran Olsen, compiler and professor of Native American music; and John Guido, head of Manuscripts and Special Collections, Holland Library, for their collaboration, and to Robert V. Smith, Vice-Provost for Research and Dean of the Graduate School; John Pierce, Dean of Sciences and Arts; Richard Hume, Chair of the Department of History; and Earl Smith, Chair of the Department of Comparative American Cultures, for extraordinary financial support and release time.

Beyond the university, an exceptional band of scholars and museum professionals willingly shared their knowledge and trade secrets with a novice curator. Betty White, Raymond DeMallie, and Kate Duncan sustained me with ongoing advice and criticism. Ted Brasser, David Brumbach, Jay P. Dolan, Mary DuPree, Jeanne Oyawin Eder, John C. Ewers, Christian Feest, and James Nason offered critical support and information. I also want to thank JoAllyn Archambault, Donald Bergmann, Susan Buchel, Gregory Campbell, Tony Campbell, Martha Cappelletti, Robert Carriker, Robert Cason, J. D. Cleaver, Barbara Coddington, Richard Conn, John Dann, Geoffrey Gamble, Conrad Graham, George Horse Capture, Bill Holm, Alvin Josephy, Jonathan King, Betty Long, Carlo Krieger, Melinda Knapp, Joanne Kudla, the McNickle Center of the Newberry Library, Lynette Miller, Toby Morantz, James Morrison, David Nicandri, Susan Near, Katherine Pettipas, Sergio Purim, Magdalene Sebastian, William

Reviewing a multi-screen video recreation of the sacred world of the Salish
Left to right: Brian Hathaway and John Jeibman of PPI, Portland, Oregon, exhibit fabricators; Richard Molinaroli, exhibition designer; and Jacqueline Peterson, project director.

Sturtevant, William Swagerty, Colin Taylor, the late Robert K. Thomas, Huguette van Gulewe, James Van Stone, Gilbert T. Vincent, John Waide, and Robin Wright for their suggestions and assistance.

Two museums served as partners in the mounting of *Sacred Encounters.* The Cheney Cowles Museum, Spokane, Washington, without much fanfare or reward, housed the early stages of assembly, conservation, and catalogue photography. I am deeply indebted to Glenn Mason, director of the Cheney Cowles Museum, and to staff members Judy Grollmus, Lynn Harrison, Larry Schoonover, and Sally Strawn. The Museum of the Rockies, Bozeman, Montana, beautifully presented the first installation of the exhibition to an enthusiastic public throughout the spring and summer of 1993. I extend my sincere gratitude to Art Wolf, director of the Museum of the Rockies, and to staff members Connie Estep, Shelley McKamey, Beth Merrick, Bonnie Sachatello, Frank Tose, Judy Weaver, and Margaret Wood.

Associate curator Laura Peers shared in the location, selection, and cataloguing of objects and drafted a large portion of the exhibition text. Her intelligence and strength kept the project on a straight path throughout the planning phase, as did the professional expertise of Carolyn Gilman and Allan Shipman. I am also indebted to Richard Molinaroli, David Fridberg, and Kathryn Lenard of Miles, Fridberg, Molinaroli, Inc., for a beautiful exhibition design; Jane Tai and Jeffrey Pavelka, for skillfully coordinating the exhibition; Jonathan Taggart, for overseeing the conservation and mounting of the collection; and to Susan Duhl, paper conservator; Jeanne Brako, Juliette De boeck, and Marianne Russell, object conservators; Sylvia Sumira, globe conservator; Rebecca Njaa, textile conservator; and PPI, the exhibition fabricator. Among the many individuals involved in the day-to-day preparation of the book and exhibition, I extend my thanks to Susan Schroeder, assistant to the director, who compiled the checklist; Eddy Sue Judy, Jean Johnson, and John Mellis for archival research; Danielle Steinmetz for photo research; Mary Watrous, Patricia Bechtel, Norma Fuentes Scott, Helen West, Greg George, Diane Triplett, and Lynda Carey for administrative support; James Stripes for bibliographical research and editorial help; Pat Hart for text editing; Ivar Nelson for preliminary book management; Allan Jokisaari for cartography; and Grey Crawford, Brian Merritt, Joe Mikuliak, Thomas Rochford, S.J., Bruce Seleym, and Bill Voxman for catalogue photography. I am also grateful to the University of Oklahoma Press for publishing and distributing the book.

The book has taken its present shape only in the last half year in the expert hands of Suzanne Kotz, the best editor with whom I have ever worked, and Katy Homans, who, with Sayre Coombs, created a fabulous design. My thanks to them and to Larry Johnson for his inspired suggestion that the book was already written in the exhibition and merely needed to be refitted to the page. He was right.

The exhibition was made possible by generous grants from the National Endowment for the Humanities, its state affiliates in Missouri, Montana, Idaho, and Washington, and the Lilly Endowment, Inc. I am grateful to the Lilly Endowment, Inc., and the L. J. Skaggs and Mary C. Skaggs Foundation for generous grants that made the book possible.

Finally, I want to thank my ever-patient family and the close friends who clung tightly with me until the dream was real.

— **Jacqueline Peterson**

On location in Montana
Standing: Jacqueline Peterson, project director; Frances Vanderburg, production assistant; Lawrence Johnson, producer. Seated: John Peter Paul, Pend Oreille elder.

Checklist of Unillustrated Objects

I. The Catholic World

Religious Medallion
France, prior to 1622
copper
1³/₁₆ x ¹¹/₁₆ (3 x 1.7)
Sainte-Marie among the
Hurons, Midland, Ontario
s267811

Constitution des Jésuites
France, 1762
3 vols., paper, ink
6⁷/₈ x 4¹/₁₆ (17.5 x 10.4)
St. Louis University Ar-
chives, Pius XII Memorial
Library, St. Louis, Rare
Book Inventory 1762.2

*Christelyke Onderwyzing
en Gebeden*
Belgium, 1767
paper, leather, silver,
poly-chrome, gold leaf,
ink
6⁵/₈ x 4¹/₈ x 1³/₄ (16.9 x
10.5 x 4.4)
Collection of Jozef Dauwe,
Lebbeke, Belgium

Sainte Marie
Paris, ca. 1800
etching on hand-laid
paper
17¹/₈ x 10¹/₂ (43.5 x 26.7)
Collection of Jozef Dauwe,
Lebbeke, Belgium

Mater Dolorosa
P. Romagnoli, Italy, 1842
copper engraving on
paper, possibly gouache
11¹¹/₁₆ x 8³/₁₆ (29.7 x 20.8)
Collection of Jozef Dauwe,
Lebbeke, Belgium

*Rosary of Our Lady
of Lourdes*
France, after 1858
wood and metal
60³/₄ x 2⁵/₁₆ (154.3 x 5.9)
Dom Bernard Daeleman
o.s.b., Dendermonde,
Belgium

Jacob's Ladder
France, 18th century
etching and engraving
on hand-laid paper,
watercolor
4¹/₂ x 6 (11.3 x 15.2)
Collection of Jozef Dauwe,
Lebbeke, Belgium

New Year's Gift
Belgium, late 18th–early
19th century
etching and engraving on
hand-laid paper
5¹/₈ x 3¹/₂ (13 x 8.8)
Collection of Jozef Dauwe,
Lebbeke, Belgium

Holy Card
19th century
ink, paper
4³/₈ x 2⁷/₈ (11.1 x 7.3)
Rare Books and Special
Collections, The Catholic
University of America Li-
brary, Washington, D.C.

*Ruins of Benedictine
Abbey, Affligem, Belgium*
unknown artist
Belgium, ca. 1814
watercolor and ink on
paper
7⁷/₈ x 10⁷/₁₆ (20 x 26.5)
Collection of Jozef Dauwe,
Lebbeke, Belgium

*Beguinage of Dender-
monde, Belgium*
Belgium, ca. 1850–1900
oil on textile
28⁷/₈ x 42¹/₂ (73.3 x 108)
V.Z.W.D. Begijnhof van
Dendermonde, Dender-
monde, Belgium 79.258.15

II. Plateau World in Transition, early 19th century

*Man's Beaded and
Fringed Shirt*
Plateau, mid-19th century
Indian tanned leather,
glass pony and seed
beads, woven textile,
sinew, thread, red ochre
34¹/₂ x 43¹/₄ (87.6 x
109.9)
Duane and Wendy Alder-
man Collection,
Pendleton, Oregon

Robert Campbell Leggings
Plains (possibly Blackfeet),
mid-19th century
Indian tanned leather,
porcupine quills, glass
pony beads, cotton,
sinew, thread, brass,
metal, and horn buttons
32 (inseam) x 16 (waist)
(81.3 x 40.6)
Campbell House Museum,
St. Louis

Charlo's Lance
Plateau (Flathead),
mid-19th century
wood, iron, Indian tanned
leather, eagle feathers,
brass tacks, rawhide,
pigment
100 x 2³/₄ (254 x 7)
Collections of the Denver
Art Museum, Museum
Purchase 1949.3659

*Ambrose and the
Blackfeet*
Ambrose (Five Crows)
Plateau (Salish),
ca. 1840–47
ink on paper
7¹/₂ x 9¹/₂ (19 x 24.1)
De Smetiana Collection,
Jesuit Missouri Province
Archives, St. Louis
IX-C4-457

War Exploit of Ambrose
Ambrose (Five Crows)
Plateau (Salish),
ca. 1840–47
ink on paper
9¹/₂ x 7¹/₂ (24.1 x 19)
De Smetiana Collection,
Jesuit Missouri Province
Archives, St. Louis
IX-C4-481

War Exploit of Ambrose
Ambrose (Five Crows)
Plateau (Salish,
ca. 1840–47)
ink on paper
9¹/₂ x 7¹/₂ (24.1 x 19)
De Smetiana Collection,
Jesuit Missouri Province
Archives, St. Louis
IX-C4-469

Snowshoes from Lorette
Northeast (Huron),
ca. 1850
wood, rawhide, metal
wire
44¹/₄ x 11⁷/₈ (112.4 x 30.2)
Missouri Historical Soci-
ety, St. Louis 66-2327

*Hudson's Bay Company
Style Trade Gun*
London, ca. 1855
walnut, hickory, iron,
brass
HBC style fusil
39 x 5³/₈ x 2³/₈ (99 x
13.7 x 6)
Samuel E. Johns Collec-
tion, Gift of S. Douglas
Johns, Montana Historical
Society, Helena, Montana
X59.06.83

III. Pierre-Jean De Smet and the Mission to the Rockies

Box with De Smet's Name
St. Louis, ca. 1830
wood, iron
15 x 28 x 6¹/₄ (38.1 x
71.3 x 15.9)
Museum of the Western
Jesuit Missions, Floris-
sant, Missouri 991.8

Thirteen-key Clarinet in C
believed to have be-
longed to De Smet
Louis-Auguste Buffet,
maker
Paris, ca. 1835
boxwood, brass, ivory,
cork, cotton
23¹/₄ x 3¹/₈ (59 x 8)
Oregon Province of the
Society of Jesus, Portland
SJ 64 A-F

Pierre Jean De Smet, S.J.,
photograph, ca. 1840
De Smetiana Collection,
Jesuit Missouri Province
Archives, St. Louis IX-H19

De Smet's Cigar Holder
America or Europe,
ca. 1840–70
leather, metal
5¹/₂ x 3¹/₄ x 1¹/₂ (14 x
8.2 x 3.8)
Museum of the Western
Jesuit Missions, Floris-
sant, Missouri 990.7 A, B

De Smet's Wine Flask
G. and J. W. Hawksley,
maker
America, mid-19th century
metal, cork
6 x 3¹/₄ x 1¹/₄ (15.2 x
8.3 x 3.1)
Museum of the Western
Jesuit Missions, Floris-
sant, Missouri 990.6 A–C

Crucifix
America?, 19th century
metal
4³/₈ x 2 (11.1 x 5.1)
Oregon Province of the
Society of Jesus, Portland
SJ 115

Bible History
D. Hale, Boston, 1814
leather, paper, ink, gilt,
thread
2 x 1³/₈ x ³/₄ (5.1 x 3.5 x
1.9)
Oregon Province of the
Society of Jesus, Portland
SJ 53

*Beaded Cover for
Bible History*
Plateau, 20th century
Indian tanned leather,
glass seed beads,
cotton thread
6⁵/₈ x 2¹/₂ x ¹/₄ (16.8 x
6.3 x .6)
Oregon Province of the
Society of Jesus, Portland
SJ 53

Candlesticks
attributed to Anthony
Ravalli, S.J.
America, 19th century
wood, paint
35 x 5 x 5 (88.9 x 12.7 x
12.7)
Old Mission State Park,
Cataldo, Idaho 110-75-1-4

Altar Cards
America, early 20th
century
paper, fabric, varnish, gilt,
ink
10¹/₄ x 6¹/₂ (26 x 17),
13 x 9³/₄ (33 x 24.8)
Sacred Heart Mission
to the Coeur d'Alene,
De Smet, Idaho

Chalice
probably America, mid-
19th century
silver, gold-plated silver
8⁷/₁₆ x 4⁷/₁₆ (21.4 x 11.3)
Oregon Province of the
Society of Jesus, Portland
SJ 70A

Chalice Case
probably America, mid-
19th century
leather, metal, paper-
board
11¹/₄ x 5⁵/₈ (28.5 x 14.3)
Oregon Province of the
Society of Jesus, Portland
SJ 70B

*Letters and Sketches,
with a Narrative of a
Year's Residence among
the Indians of the Rocky
Mountains*
Pierre-Jean De Smet
Philadelphia, M. Fithian,
1843
paper, cloth, gilt, ink
7³/₄ x 4⁷/₈ (19.7 x 12.4)
Washington State Univer-
sity Libraries, Pullman
F 592.S63

*Viaggi alle Montagne
Rocciose de P. Pietro
de Smet, missionario
D.C.D.G.*
Pierre-Jean De Smet,
translated by Francese da
Luigi Previte, D.M.C.
Palermo, dalla Stamperia
di Francesco Lao, 1847
paper, paperboard, ink
7³/₈ x 4¹/₂ (18 x 11.5)
St. Louis University Ar-
chives, Pius XII Memorial
Library F 592.S65 1847

Missions de l'Oregon et Voyages dans les Montagnes Rocheuses en 1845 et 1846
Pierre-Jean De Smet
Paris, Librairie de Poussielgue-Rusand, 1848
paper, leather, gilt, ink
$7^1/4$ x $4^5/8$ (18.4 x 11.8)
Washington State University Libraries, Pullman
F80.S644 1848

Pierre-Jean De Smet
photograph, ca. 1855
De Smetiana Collection, J. E. Windey, S.J., Brussels
NR 97

IV. The Surrounded: The Reservation Era

Springfield Rifle with Cross Inlay
Plateau (Nez Perce), ca. 1870
wood, iron, pewter or lead inlay
$4^1/2$ x $1^3/4$ x $45^1/2$ (11.5 x 4.5 x 150.6)
Cheney Cowles Museum, Spokane, Washington
529.1

Flathead Indian Flute
St. Ignatius Mission, Montana, ca. 1890
wood (possibly elderberry), cork
$11^1/4$ x $7/8$ (28.5 x 2.2)
Oregon Province of the Society of Jesus, Portland
GU 331

Flathead Indian Agency
photograph, 1884
Haynes Foundation Collection, Montana Historical Society, Helena H-2007

Burning Infected Tipis
photograph, 1901
Oregon Province Archives of the Society of Jesus, Crosby Library, Gonzaga University, Spokane, Washington OPA LESHER COLLECTION

Peter Campbell's House
photograph, late 19th–early 20th century
Coeur d'Alene Tribe, Historical Testimony Program, De Smet, Idaho

Gambling Bag and Bones
Plateau, late 19th century–early 20th century
natural fiber, corn husk, wool, cotton, wool yarn, thread, Indian tanned leather, bone
bag: $8^3/4$ x $5^1/2$ x $5/8$ (22.2 x 14 x 1.9), bones: $2^1/2$ x dia.$7/8$ (6.5 x 2.2)
Cheney Cowles Museum, Spokane, Washington
KING 1970 #99

Flathead Doll on Horse
Plateau (Salish), ca. 1900
Indian tanned leather, wool, cotton, glass seed beads, horsehair, paint, thread, leather
doll: $6^3/4$ x $4^1/2$ x 2 (17 x 11.5 x 4.8), horse: $5^3/4$ x $2^3/4$ x 8 (14.5 x 7 x 20.5)
Montana Historical Society, Museum Collection, Helena X82.38.02 A-C

V. Drawings by Nicolas Point, S.J.

Unless otherwise indicated, the drawings, all made in America, date ca. 1841–47 and are ink on paper

Moving the Lodge
$4^1/4$ x $6^1/2$ (10.8 x 16.5)
De Smetiana Collection, Jesuit Missouri Province Archives, St. Louis
IX-C9-86

Details of a Hunt
$4^1/2$ x 7 (11.4 x 17.8)
De Smetiana Collection, Jesuit Missouri Province Archives, St. Louis
IX-C9-98

Discovery of the Buffalo
graphite and ink on paper
$4^1/4$ x 7 (10.8 x 17.8)
Pierre Jean De Smet Papers, Washington State University Libraries, Pullman 537.7.34.55

Chief Victor Defends Himself against a Blackfeet Camp
$4^1/2$ x $7^1/2$ (11.4 x 19.1)
De Smetiana Collection, Jesuit Missouri Province Archives, St. Louis
IX-C9-71

War Exploit of Victor
$4^1/2$ x $7^1/4$ (11.4 x 18.4)
De Smetiana Collection, Jesuit Missouri Province Archives, St. Louis
IX-C9-72

Missionary and Child in Missionaries' Cabin
watercolor in black on paper, ca. 1841–46
$4^1/8$ x 7 (10.5 x 17.8)
De Smetiana Collection, Jesuit Missouri Province Archives, St. Louis
IX-C9-57

War Exploit of Smoiré
5 x $7^7/8$ (12.7 x 20.1)
De Smetiana Collection, Jesuit Missouri Province Archives, St. Louis
IX-C9-76

Children at Play
4 x $6^1/2$ (10.2 x 16.5)
De Smetiana Collection, Jesuit Missouri Province Archives, St. Louis
IX-C9-93

Meeting of Two Friends
$4^1/4$ x $6^1/2$ (10.8 x 16.5)
De Smetiana Collection, Jesuit Missouri Province Archives, St. Louis
IX-C9-87

Announcement of the Discovery of Buffalo
graphite and ink on paper
$4^3/8$ x 7 (11.1 x 17.8)
Pierre Jean De Smet Papers, Washington State University Libraries, Pullman 537.7.35.56

Sioux Family, Very Friendly to the Whites
graphite on paper, ca. 1841
$3^1/4$ x 6 (8.3 x 15.2)
Pierre Jean De Smet Papers, Washington State University Libraries, Pullman 537.7.24.38

Devil's Gate
graphite and ink on paper, ca. 1841
4 x $6^7/8$ (10.2 x 17.5)
De Smetiana Collection, Jesuit Missouri Province Archives, St. Louis
IX-C9-39

Michel par son frère François de Gissar
graphite on paper, ca. 1841–42
$8^3/8$ x $6^1/2$ (21.3 x 16.5)
Pierre Jean De Smet Papers, Washington State University Libraries, Pullman 537.7.38.59

Tintennemi (Michel)
graphite on paper, ca. 1842
$7^1/4$ x $4^3/4$ (18.4 x 12.1)
De Smetiana Collection, Jesuit Missouri Province Archives, St. Louis
IX-C9-14

Ignace (Etienne)
ca. 1842
each $3^3/4$ x 5 (9.5 x 12.7)
De Smetiana Collection, Jesuit Missouri Province Archives, St. Louis
IX-C9-17 A,B

Portrait of an Unidentified Indian
graphite on paper, ca. 1842
$7^1/8$ x 5 (18.1 x 12.7)
De Smetiana Collection, Jesuit Missouri Province Archives, St. Louis
IX-C9-13

The Land of Ignace as Viewed from the South
ca. 1842
$4^1/4$ x $7^1/4$ (10.8 x 18.4)
De Smetiana Collection, Jesuit Missouri Province Archives, St. Louis
IX-C9-20

The Baptism of Ignace by Father De Smet
ca. 1842
$4^1/2$ x $7^1/4$ (11.4 x 18.4)
De Smetiana Collection, Jesuit Missouri Province Archives, St. Louis
IX-C9-23

Praying before Getting Under Way
ca. 1841–47
$4^1/2$ x $6^1/2$ (11.4 x 16.5)
De Smetiana Collection, Jesuit Missouri Province Archives, St. Louis
IX-C9-84

Communion
$4^5/8$ x $7^3/8$ (11.8 x 18.7)
De Smetiana Collection, Jesuit Missouri Province Archives, St. Louis
IX-C9-96

The Power of the Cross to Cure Illness
watercolor on paper
4 x $6^7/8$ (10.2 x 17.5)
De Smetiana Collection, Jesuit Missouri Province Archives, St. Louis
IX-C9-56

Report of the Great Chief
graphite and ink on paper, ca. 1841–46
5 x $7^1/8$ (12.7 x 18.1)
Pierre Jean De Smet Papers, Washington State University Libraries, Pullman 537.7.36.57

The Sacrament of Last Rites Given to Ignace
ca. 1842
$4^1/2$ x 7 (11.4 x 17.8)
De Smetiana Collection, Jesuit Missouri Province Archives, St. Louis
IX-C9-25

Morning Prayer
ca. 1841–46
$4^3/8$ x $6^3/8$ (11.1 x 16.2)
De Smetiana Collection, Jesuit Missouri Province Archives, St. Louis
IX-C9-83

Etienne's Vision
ca. 1842–46
$4^1/4$ x 7 (10.8 x 17.8)
De Smetiana Collection, Jesuit Missouri Province Archives, St. Louis
IX-C9-21

Pierre Jean (Le Petit Faro)
ca. 1841–46
7 x $4^1/2$ (17.8 x 11.4)
De Smetiana Collection, Jesuit Missouri Province Archives, St. Louis
IX-C9-8

VI. Maps

Segment of Map of the Missouri River from the Mouth of the Platte to the Vermillion River
Pierre-Jean De Smet
ink on paper, ca. 1833–39
Each sheet $15^1/2$ x $12^1/2$ (39.4 x 31.8)
De Smetiana Collection, Jesuit Missouri Province Archives, St. Louis
IX-C8-11

Victor's Map of Roothaan Lake
Victor
Plateau (Kalispel), ca. 1842–48
graphite on paper
7 x $8^3/4$ (17.8 x 22.2)
De Smetiana Collection, Jesuit Missouri Province Archives, St. Louis
IX-C8-35

Spokane, Clark, and Kootenay Rivers
Pierre-Jean De Smet
ink on paper, ca. 1842–48
$20^1/2$ x $23^1/4$ (52.1 x 60.3)
De Smetiana Collection, Jesuit Missouri Province Archives, St. Louis
IX-C8-27

Map of "Great Interior Basin of California"
Pierre-Jean De Smet
colored ink on paper, ca. 1842–58
20 x 24 (50.8 x 61)
De Smetiana Collection, Jesuit Missouri Province Archives, St. Louis
IX-C8-1

Map of Oregon Territory in 1846
Pierre-Jean De Smet
colored ink on paper, 1846
$8^1/2$ x $10^1/4$ (21.6 x 26)
De Smetiana Collection, Jesuit Missouri Province Archives, St. Louis
IX-C8-16

Lenders to the Exhibition

Alabama Department of Archives and History, Montgomery

Duane and Wendy Alderman, Pendleton, Oregon

Anonymous, Belgium

Buffalo Bill Historical Center, Cody, Wyoming

Campbell House Museum, St. Louis

The Catholic University, Washington, D.C.

Cheney Cowles Museum, Spokane, Washington

Dom Bernard Daeleman, o.s.b., Dendermonde, Belgium

Jozef Dauwe, Lebbeke, Belgium

Denver Art Museum

The Thaw Collection, courtesy New York State Historical Association, Cooperstown

John C. Ewers, Arlington, Virginia

Field Museum of Natural History, Chicago

Four Winds Indian Trading Post, St. Ignatius, Montana

Jesuit Missouri Province Archives, St. Louis

Kerkfabriek Onze-Lieve-Vrouwekerk, Dendermonde, Belgium

McCord Museum of Canadian History, Montreal

Manitoba Museum of Man and Nature, Winnipeg

Maryhill Museum of Art, Goldendale, Washington

Minnesota Historical Society, St. Paul

Missouri Historical Society, St. Louis

Montana Historical Society, Helena

Museum of the Western Jesuit Missions, Florissant, Missouri

National Museum of Natural History, Smithsonian Institution, Washington, D.C.

Nez Perce National Historic Park, Spalding, Idaho

Ohio Historical Society, Columbus

Old Mission State Park, Cataldo, Idaho

Oregon Historical Society, Portland

Oregon Province of the Society of Jesus, Portland

Sacred Heart Mission to the Coeur d'Alene, De Smet, Idaho

St. Louis University, Pius XII Memorial Library

Sainte-Marie among the Hurons, Midland, Ontario

Snite Museum of Art, University of Notre Dame, Indiana

State Historical Society of North Dakota, Bismarck

Stedelijke Musea, Dendermonde, Belgium

University of Michigan, William L. Clements Library, Ann Arbor

University of Montana, Ethnographic Collections, Missoula

V.Z.W.D. Begijnhof van Dendermonde, Dendermonde, Belgium

Washington State University Libraries, Pullman

Lenders of Exhibition Graphics

American Antiquarian Society, Worcester, Massachusetts

Archief Noordbelgische Jezuitenprovincie, Heverlee, Belgium

Archives des Jésuites, St-Jérôme, Québec

Bibliothèque Nationale, Paris

Bitterroot Valley Historical Society, Hamilton, Montana

Cathédrale Notre Dame de Chartres, France

Cupples House, St. Louis

Church Council of Greater Seattle, Native American Task Force

Denver Public Library

Lucylle Evans, Stevensville, Montana

Historic Testimony Program, Coeur d'Alene Tribe, DeSmet, Idaho

Hudson's Bay Company Archives, Provincial Archives of Manitoba, Winnipeg, Manitoba

Loyola University Press, Chicago

National Anthropological Archives, Smithsonian Institution, Washington, D.C.

National Archives of Canada, Ottawa

National Archives and Records Administration, Washington, D.C.

Österreichische Nationalbibliothek, Vienna

Zisterzienserstift Zwettl Bibliothek, Stift Zwettl, Austria

Spokane Public Library, Washington

Stark Museum of Art, Orange, Texas

Pierre Van de Velde, Moortsele, Belgium

Washington State Historical Society, Tacoma

Bibliography

Allen, John L. "Patterns of Promise: Mapping the Plains and Prairies, 1800–1860." In *Mapping the North American Plains: Essays in the History of Cartography*, ed. Frederick C. Luebke, Frances W. Kaye, and Gary E. Moulton, 41–62. Norman: University of Oklahoma Press with the Center for Great Plains Studies, University of Nebraska-Lincoln, 1987.

Anastasio, Angelo. "The Southern Plateau: An Ecological Analysis of Intergroup Relations." *Northwest Anthropological Research Notes* 6 (1972): 109–229.

Axtell, James. *The Invasion Within: The Contest of Cultures in Colonial North America.* New York: Oxford University Press, 1985.

_____. "Preachers, Priests, and Pagans: Catholic and Protestant Missions in Colonial North America." In *New Dimensions in Ethnohistory: Papers of the Second Laurier Conference on Ethnohistory and Ethnology*, ed. Barry Gough and Laird Christie, 65–78. Quebec: Canadian Museum of Civilization, 1991.

Bangert, William V. *A History of the Society of Jesus.* Rev. ed. St. Louis: Institute of Jesuit Sources, 1986.

Bidwell, John. *A Journey to California, 1841: The First Emigrant Party to California by Wagon Train: The Journal of John Bidwell.* 1843. Reprint. Berkeley: Friends of the Bancroft Library, 1964.

Bigart, Robert, and Clarence Woodcock. "St. Ignatius Mission, Montana: Reports from Two Jesuit Missionaries, 1885 and 1900–1901." *Arizona and the West* 23 (1981): 149–72, 267–78.

Blanchet, Francis Norbert. *Historical Sketches of the Catholic Church in Oregon.* 1878. Reprint. Ed. Edward J. Kowrach. Fairfield, Wash.: Ye Galleon Press, 1983.

Boas, Franz. *Kutenai Tales.* Bureau of American Ethnology Bulletin, no. 59. Washington, D.C.: Government Printing Office, 1918.

Brown, Ellsworth H. "The History of the Flathead Indians in the Nineteenth Century." Ph.D. diss. Michigan State University, East Lansing, 1975.

Brumbach, David M. "Peter John De Smet, S.J.: Fundraiser and Promoter of Missions." Ph.D. diss. Washington State University, Pullman, 1992.

Buckley, Cornelius M. *Nicolas Point, S.J.: His Life and Northwest Indian Chronicles.* Chicago: Loyola University Press, 1989.

Burns, Robert. "A Jesuit at the Hellgate Treaty of 1855." *Mid-America* 34 (1952): 87–114.

_____. *The Jesuits and the Indian Wars of the Northwest.* New Haven: Yale University Press, 1966. Reprint. Moscow: University of Idaho Press, 1986.

Campeau, Lucien. "Roman Catholic Missions in New France." In *History of Indian-White Relations*, ed. Wilcomb E. Washburn, 464–71. Vol. 4 of *Handbook of North American Indians*, ed. William C. Sturtevant. Washington, D.C.: Smithsonian Institution, 1988.

Caraman, Philip. *The Lost Paradise: The Jesuit Reductions in Paraguay.* Notre Dame: University of Notre Dame Press, 1975.

Carrol, James. "Flatheads and Whites: A Study of Conflict." Ph.D. diss. University of California, Berkeley, 1959.

Chance, David H. "Influences of the Hudson's Bay Company on the Native Cultures of the Colville District." *Northwest Anthropological Research Notes* 7, no. 2 (1973): 33–127.

Châtellier, Louis. *The Europe of the Devout: The Catholic Reformation and the Formation of a New Society.* Trans. Jean Birrell. Cambridge: Cambridge University Press, 1989.

Chittenden, Hiram Martin. *The American Fur Trade of the Far West: A History of the Pioneer Trading Posts and Early Fur Companies of the Missouri Valley and the Rocky Mountains and of the Overland Commerce with Santa Fe.* 3 vols. New York: Francis P. Harper, 1902.

Chittenden, Hiram Martin, and Alfred Talbot Richardson. *Life, Letters and Travels of Father Pierre-Jean De Smet, S.J., 1801–1873.* 4 vols. New York: Francis P. Harper, 1905. Reprint. New York: Arno Press and the New York Times, 1969.

Connolly, Thomas E., ed. *Quay-Lem u En-Chow-Men: A Collection of Hymns and Prayers in Flathead–Kalispel–Spokane Indian Language.* Worley, Id.: Mitch Michael, 1958.

Curtis, Edward S. "Salishan Tribes of the Interior: Flatheads and Pend d'Oreilles." In *The North American Indian*, vol. 7, 43–189. 1911. Reprint. New York: Johnson Reprint, 1970.

Davis, W. L. *A History of St. Ignatius Mission.* Spokane: C. W. Hill Printing, 1954.

_____. "Peter John De Smet: The Journey of 1840." *Pacific Northwest Quarterly* 35 (1944): 29–43.

Denig, Edwin Thompson. *Five Indian Tribes of the Upper Missouri.* Ed. John C. Ewers. Norman: University of Oklahoma Press, 1961.

De Smet, P.J. *Cinquante Nouvelles Lettres.* Paris and Tournai: H. Casterman, 1858; also published as *Western Missions and Missionaries: A Series of Letters.* New York: P. J. Kenedy, 1859. Reprint. New York: James B. Kirker, 1863.

_____. "Father De Smet's Narrative Describing Upper Washington Territory, 1859." *American Catholic Historical Researches* 12, no. 3 (1859): 102–106.

_____. *The Indian Missions in the United States of America under the Care of the Missouri Province of the Society of Jesus.* Philadelphia: King and Baird, 1841.

_____. *Letters and Sketches: with a Narrative of a Year's Residence among the Indian Tribes of the Rocky Mountains.* Philadelphia: M. Fithian, 1843.

_____. *New Indian Sketches.* Boston: D. and J. Sadlier, 1863.

_____. *Oregon Missions and Travels over the Rocky Mountains in 1845–46.* New York: E. Dunigan, 1847. Vol. 27 of *Early Western Travels*, ed. Reuben Gold Thwaites. Cleveland: Arthur H. Clark, 1906. Reprint. Fairfield, Wash.: Ye Galleon Press, 1978.

_____. *Origins, Progress, and Prospects of the Catholic Mission to the Rocky Mountains.* Philadelphia: M. Fithian, 1843.

_____. *Voyage au Grand Desert en 1851.* Brussels: Imprimerie de J. Vandereydt, 1853.

Diomedi, Alexander. *Sketches of Indian Life in the Pacific Northwest.* Ed. Edward J. Kowrach. Fairfield, Wash.: Ye Galleon Press, 1978.

Dolan, Jay P. *The American Catholic Experience: A History from Colonial Times to the Present.* New York: Doubleday, 1985.

Drury, Clifford M. *Henry Harmon Spalding: Pioneer of Old Oregon.* Caldwell, Id.: Caxton Printers, 1936.

_____. *Nine Years with the Spokane Indians: The Diary, 1838–1848, of Elkanah Walker.* Glendale, Calif.: Arthur A. Clark, 1976.

Duratschek, Mary Claudia. *Crusading along Sioux Trails: A History of the Catholic Indian Missions of South Dakota.* St. Meinrad, Ind.: The Grail, 1947.

Dusenberry, J. Verne. "Sample of Pend d'Orielle Oral Literature and Salish Narratives." In *Life-ways of Intermontane and Plains Montana Indians*, ed. Leslie B. Davis, 109–20. Occasional Papers of the Museum of the Rockies, no. 1. Bozeman: Museum of the Rockies and Montana State University Press, 1979.

Evans, Lucylle H. *St. Mary's in the Rocky Mountains.* Stevensville: Montana Creative Consultants, 1976.

Ewers, John C. *Gustavus Sohon's Portrait of Flathead and Pend d'Orielle Indians, 1854.* Smithsonian Miscellaneous Collections, vol. 110, no. 7. Washington, D.C.: Smithsonian Institution, 1948.

_____. "Iroquois Indians in the Far West." *Montana Magazine of Western History* 13 (1963): 2–10.

_____. "A Unique Pictorial Interpretation of Blackfoot Indian Religion in 1846–47." *Ethnohistory* 18 (1972): 231–38.

Fahey, John. *The Flathead Indians.* Norman: University of Oklahoma Press, 1974.

_____. *The Kalispel Indians.* Norman: University of Oklahoma Press, 1986.

Farr, William E. *The Reservation Blackfeet, 1882–1945: A Photographic History of Cultural Survival.* Seattle: University of Washington Press, 1984.

Flathead Culture Committee. *A Brief History of the Flathead Tribes.* 3d ed. St. Ignatius, Mont.: Flathead Culture Committee of the Confederated Salish and Kootenai Tribes, 1983.

Forbis, R. G. "Religious Acculturation of the Flathead Indians of Montana." M.A. thesis, Montana State University, Bozeman, 1950.

Frison, George C. *Prehistoric Hunters of the High Plains.* New York: Academic Press, 1978.

Ganss, George E., ed. *Ignatius of Loyola: The Spiritual Exercises and Selected Works.* Classics of Western Spirituality. New York: Paulist Press, 1991.

_____, trans. *The Constitution of the Society of Jesus.* Ignatius of Loyala. St. Louis: Institute of Jesuit Sources, 1970.

_____, trans. *The Spiritual Exercises of Saint Ignatius: A Translation and Commentary.* St. Louis: Institute of Jesuit Sources, 1992.

Garfield, James A. "Report of Hon. James A. Garfield, Commissioner for Removal of the Flathead Tribe of Indians from the Bitter Root Valley, in Montana Territory, to the Jocko Reservation, in Said Territory, with Accompanying Papers." In *Fourth Annual Report of the Board of Indian Commissioners, 1872, 109–18.* Washington, D.C.: Government Printing Office, 1873.

Garraghan, Gilbert J. *The Jesuits of the Middle United States.* 3 vols. New York: America Press, 1938. Reprint. Chicago: Loyola University Press, 1983.

Garth, Thomas R. "The Plateau Whipping Complex and its Relationship to Plateau-Southwest Contacts." *Ethnohistory* 12 (1965): 141–71.

Gibson, Ralph. *A Social History of French Catholicism 1789–1914.* London: Routledge, 1989.

Gillett, Gary Lee. *A Musical History of the St. Mary's Mission Community, 1841–1891.* M.M.E. thesis, University of Montana, Missoula, 1987.

Giorda, J[oseph], et al., comp. *A Dictionary of the Kalispel or Flathead Indian Language.* 2 vols. St. Ignatius, Mont.: St. Ignatius Press, 1877–79.

Goldsmith, Jane ten Brink. "Jesuit Iconography: the Evolution of the Visual Idiom." In *Jesuit Art in North American Collections,* ed. Goldsmith et al., 16–21. Dobbs Ferry, N.Y.: Patrick and Beatrice Haggerty Museum of Art, Marquette University, 1991.

Grant, John Webster. *Moon of Wintertime: Missionaries and the Indians of Canada in Encounter since 1534.* Toronto: University of Toronto Press, 1984.

Guibert, Joseph de. *The Jesuits: Their Spiritual Doctrine and Practice.* Trans. William J. Young. St. Louis and Chicago: Institute of Jesuit Sources and Loyola University Press, 1964.

Harrod, Howard L. *Mission among the Blackfeet.* Norman: University of Oklahoma Press, 1971.

Heidenreich, Conrad E. "Huron." In *Northeast,* ed. Bruce G. Trigger, 368–88. Vol. 15 of *Handbook of North American Indians,* ed. William C. Sturtevant. Washington, D.C.: Smithsonian Institution, 1978.

Hill-Tout, Charles. *The Thompson and Okanagan.* Vol. 1 of *The Salish People: The Local Contribution of Charles Hill-Tout,* ed. Ralph Maud. Vancouver: Talonbooks, 1978.

Horse Capture, George P., and Richard A. Pohrt. *Salish Indian Art from the J. R. Simplot Collection.* Cody, Wyo.: Buffalo Bill Historical Center, 1986.

Hoyt, C. Eugene. "The Good Friday Service at the St. Ignatius Mission, Montana." M.A. thesis, Montana State University, Bozeman, 1952.

Hungry Wolf, Adolf. *Charlo's People: The Flathead Tribe of Montana.* Invermere, B.C.: Good Medicine Books, 1974.

Jaenen, Cornelius. *Friend and Foe: Aspects of French-Amerindian Cultural Contact in the Sixteenth and Seventeenth Centuries.* New York: Columbia University Press, 1976.

_____. *The Role of the Church in New France.* Toronto: McGraw-Hill Ryerson, 1976.

Johnson, Olga Weydemeyer. *Flathead and Kootenay: The Rivers, the Tribes and the Region's Traders.* Glendale, Calif.: Arthur A. Clark, 1969.

Josephy, Alvin. *The Nez Perce Indians and the Opening of the Northwest.* New Haven: Yale University Press, 1965.

Keyser, James D. *Indian Rock Art of the Columbia Plateau.* Seattle: University of Washington Press, 1992.

Kselman, Thomas A. *Miracles and Prophecies in Nineteenth Century France.* New Brunswick: Rutgers University Press, 1983.

Lanternari, Vittorio. *The Religions of the Oppressed: A Study of Modern Messianic Cults.* Trans. Lisa Sergio. New York: New American Library, 1963.

Laveille, E. *The Life of Father De Smet, S.J.* Reprint. Chicago: Loyola University Press, 1981.

Lécrivain, Philippe. *Pour une plus grande gloire de Dieu: Les missions jesuites.* Paris: Decouvertes Gallimard, 1991.

Lucas, Thomas M., ed. *Saint, Site, and Sacred Strategy: Ignatius Rome and Jesuit Urbanism.* Vatican City: Biblioteca Apostolica Vaticana, 1990.

McDonough, Peter. *Men Astutely Trained: A History of the Jesuits in the American Century.* New York: Free Press, 1992.

McKevitt, Gerald. "Gregorio Mengarini, 1811–1886, North American Missionary and Linguist." *Archivum Historicum* 61 (1992): 171–88.

Malouf, Carling. "Economy and Land Use by the Indians of Western Montana." In *Interior Salish and Eastern Washington Indians II,* ed. Stuart A. Chalfant et al., 117–78. New York: Garland Publishing, 1974.

Markowitz, Harvey. "The Catholic Mission and the Sioux: A Crisis in the Early Paradigm." In *Sioux Indian Religion: Tradition and Innovation,* ed. Raymond J. DeMallie and Douglas R. Parks, 113–37. Norman: University of Oklahoma Press, 1987.

Mengarini, Gregory. *Recollections of the Flathead Mission.* Trans. Gloria Ricci Lothrop. Glendale, Calif.: Arthur H. Clark, 1977.

_____. "The Rocky Mountains: Memoirs of Fr. Gregory Mengarini." *Woodstock Letters* 17 (1888): 298–309; 18 (1889): 142–52. Reprint. Albert J. Partoll, ed. "Mengarini's Narrative of the Rockies: Memoirs of Old Oregon, 1841, and St. Mary's Mission." In *Frontier Omnibus,* ed. John W. Hakola, 139–60. Missoula: Montana State University Press, 1962.

_____. *Salish or Flathead Grammar.* New York: Cramoisy Press, 1861.

Merriam, Alan P. *Ethnomusicology of the Flathead Indians.* Viking Fund Publications in Anthropology, vol. 44. Chicago: Aldine, 1967.

_____. "The Importance of Song in the Flathead Indian Vision Quest." *Ethnomusicology* 9, no. 2 (1965): 91–99.

_____. "The Use of Music in the Study of a Problem of Acculturation." *American Anthropologist* 57 (1955): 28–34.

McNaspy, Cornelius J. *Lost Cities of Paraguay: Art and Architecture of the Jesuit Reductions 1607–1767.* Chicago: Loyola University Press, 1982.

McNickle, D'Arcy. *The Surrounded.* 1936. Reprint. Albuquerque: University of New Mexico Press, 1964.

Major-Frégeau, Madeleine, ed. *Overland to Oregon in 1845: Impressions of a Journey across North America by H. J. Warre.* Ottawa: Public Archives of Canada, 1976.

Miller, Christopher L. *Prophetic Worlds: Indians and Whites of the Columbia Plateau.* New Brunswick: Rutgers University Press, 1985.

Morissonneau, Christian. "Huron of Lorette." In *Northeast,* ed. Bruce G. Trigger, 389–93. Vol. 15 of *Handbook of North American Indians,* ed. William C. Sturtevant. Washington, D.C.: Smithsonian Institution, 1978.

Morrison, Kenneth M. "Baptism and Alliance: The Symbolic Meditations of Religious Syncretism." *Ethnohistory* 37 (1990): 416–37.

Muratori, Lodovico Antonio. *Cristianesimo felice nelle missioni de' Padri della Compagnia di Gesù nel Paraguai.* 2 vols. Venice: Presso Giambatista Pasquali, 1743. French trans. *Relation des missions du Paraguai.* Louvain: Vanlinthout and Vandenzande, 1822.

O'Connor, James. "The Flathead Indians." *Records of the American Catholic Historical Society of Philadelphia* 3 (1888–91): 85–110.

Palladino, Lawrence B. *Indian and White in the Northwest.* Baltimore: John Murphy, 1894.

Parker, Samuel. *Journal of an Exploring Tour beyond the Rocky Mountains*. Ithaca, N.Y.: By the author, Mack, Andrews and Woodruff, Printers, 1838.

Partoll, Albert J., ed. "The Flathead Indian Treaty Council of 1855." *Pacific Northwest Quarterly* 29 (1938): 283–314.

Peltier, Jerome. *A Brief History of the Coeur d'Alene Indians, 1805–1909*. Fairfield, Wash.: Ye Galleon Press, 1982.

Pfaller, Louis. *Father De Smet in Dakota*. Richardton, N.D.: Assumption Abbey Press, 1962.

Point, Nicolas. "Recollections of the Rocky Mountains." *Woodstock Letters* 11 (1882): 298–321; 12 (1883): 3–22, 133–53, 261–68; 13 (1884): 3–13.

———. *Wilderness Kingdom. Indian Life in the Rocky Mountains: 1840–1847; The Journal and Paintings of Nicolas Point, S.J.* Trans. Joseph P. Donnelly. New York: Holt, Rinehart and Winston, 1967.

Point, Pierre. "Vie du Père Nicolas Point, S.J." MS in the Archives des Jésuites, St-Jérôme, Québec, Canada, AS-JSJ, no. 4073.

Prucha, Francis Paul. *American Indian Policy in Crisis: Christian Reformers and the Indian, 1865–1900*. Norman: University of Oklahoma Press, 1976.

Ramsey, Jarold. *Reading the Fire: Essay in the Traditional Indian Literatures of the Far West*. Lincoln: University of Nebraska Press, 1983.

Raufer, Maria Ilma. *Black Robes and Indians on the Last Frontier: A Story of Heroism*. Milwaukee: Bruce Publishing, 1966.

Ray, Verne. *Cultural Relations in the Plateau of Northwestern America*. Los Angeles: Southwest Museum, 1939.

Ronan, Mary. *Historical Sketch of the Flathead Indian Nation from the Year 1813 to 1890*. Helena: Journal Publishing, 1890.

Ross, Alexander. *Adventures of the First Settlers on the Oregon or Columbia River*. London: Smith, Elder and Co., 1849. Reprint. Ed. Milo Milton Quaife. Chicago: The Lakeside Press, 1923.

Rothensteiner, John. "The Flat-head and Nez Perce Delegation to St. Louis 1831–1839." *St. Louis Catholic Historical Review* 2 (1920): 183–97.

Ruby, Robert H., and John A. Brown. *Dreamer-Prophets of the Columbia Plateau: Smohalla and Skolaskin*. Norman: University of Oklahoma Press, 1989.

———. *A Guide to the Indian Tribes of the Pacific Northwest*. Norman: University of Oklahoma Press, 1986.

Ruggles, Richard I. *A Country So Interesting: The Hudson's Bay Company and Two Centuries of Mapping, 1670–1870*. Montreal and Kingston: McGill-Queen's University Press, 1991.

Schaeffer, Claude E. "An Acculturation Study of the Indians of the Flathead Reservation of Western Montana." Report to the U.S. Commissioner of Indian Affairs, ca. 1935. Department of Interior Library, Washington, D.C.

———. "The First Jesuit Mission to the Flathead, 1840–1850: A Study in Culture Conflicts." *Pacific Northwest Quarterly* 28 (1937): 227–50.

Schoenberg, Wilfred. *A Chronicle of the Catholic History of the Pacific Northwest, 1743–1960*. Portland: Catholic Sentinel Printery, 1962.

———. *Jesuits in Montana, 1840–1960*. Portland: The Oregon-Jesuit, 1960.

Smith, Burton M. "The Politics of Allotment: The Flathead Indian Reservation as a Test Case." *Pacific Northwest Quarterly* 70 (1979): 131–40.

Steinmetz, Paul B. *Pipe, Bible, and Peyote among the Oglala Lakota: A Study in Religious Identity*. Knoxville: University of Tennessee Press, 1990.

Stroobants, A[imé]. *Dendermonde, schets van een stadsgeschiedenis*. Dendermonde, 1986.

———. *Devotieprenten op perkament*. Dendermonde, 1991.

Swagerty, William. "Indian Trade in the Trans-Mississippi West to 1870." In *History of Indian White Relations*, ed. Wilcomb E. Washburn, 351–74. Vol. 4 of *Handbook of North American Indians*, ed. William C. Sturtevant. Washington, D.C.: Smithsonian Institution, 1988.

Taylor, John F. "Sociocultural Effects of Epidemics on the Northern Plains, 1734–1850." *Western Canadian Journal of Anthropology* 7, no. 4 (1977): 55–81.

Teit, James A. *The Middle Columbia Salish*. Ed. Franz Boas. University of Washington Publications in Anthropology, vol. 4. Seattle: University of Washington Press, 1928.

———. "The Salishan Tribes of the Western Plateaus." Ed. Franz Boas. *Annual Report of the Bureau of American Ethnology* 45 (1927–28): 23–396.

Thwaites, Reuben Gold, ed. *The Jesuit Relations and Allied Documents*. 73 vols. Cleveland: Burrows Bros., 1896–1901.

Trigger, Bruce G. *The Children of Aataentsic: A History of the Huron People to 1660*. 2 vols. Montreal: McGill-Queen's University Press, 1976.

———. *Natives and Newcomers: Canada's "Heroic Age" Reconsidered*. Kingston: McGill-Queen's University Press, 1985.

Trosper, Ronald L. "The Economic Impact of the Allotment Policy on the Flathead Indian Reservation." Ph.D. diss., Harvard University, 1974.

Truettner, William H. *The Natural Man Observed: A Study of Catlin's Indian Gallery*. Washington, D.C.: Smithsonian Institution Press, 1979.

Turney-High, Harry Holbert. "The Flathead Indians of Montana." *Memoirs of the American Anthropological Association*, no. 48 (1937).

Twohy, Patrick J. *Finding a Way Home: Indian and Catholic Spiritual Paths of the Plateau Tribes*. Spokane: University Press, 1983.

Vanderburg, Agnes. "Coming Back Slow." *Parabola: The Magazine of Myth and Tradition* 5, no. 1 (1980): 20–23.

Vecsey, Christopher, ed. *Handbook of American Indian Religious Freedom*. New York: Crossroad, 1991.

Vestal, Stanley. *Sitting Bull: Champion of the Sioux*. 1932. New ed. Norman: University of Oklahoma Press, 1957.

Walker, Deward E., Jr. *Conflict and Schism in Nez Perce Acculturation: A Study of Religion and Politics*. Pullman: Washington State University Press, 1968.

White, M. Catherine, ed. *David Thompson's Journals Relating to Montana and Adjacent Regions, 1808–1812*. Missoula: Montana State University Press, 1950.

White, Elizabeth L. "Adult Education and Cultural Invasion: A Case Study of the Salish and the Jesuits." Ph.D. diss., Montana State University, Bozeman, 1990.

Wilkes, Charles. *Narrative of the United States Exploring Expedition*, vol. 4. Philadelphia: Lee and Blanchard, 1845.

Windey, J.E. *Machetakonia: Pater Pieter Jan De Smet van Dendermonde bij de Indianen en de Amerikanen*. Dendermonde: Drukkerij De Hauwere-Huau, 1984.

Wright, Robin K., ed. *A Time of Gathering: Native Heritage in Washington State*. Seattle: Burke Museum and University of Washington Press, 1991.

Index